*The Forgotten
Feminine*

The Forgotten Feminine

Denise Jordan

Fatherheart Ministries
PO Box 1039, Taupo, 3351
www.fatherheart.net

Layout and prepress: wordsndesign.co.nz, Lower Hutt
Printed by TruePress, Grenada North, Wellington

ISBN 978-0-9941016-0-0

To Dorothy and Jack Winter

Contents

vii

Acknowledgements

It was my intention to have this book in print by the end of 2007, but however well intentioned I was, it has taken until now to finally get it to print. The ensuing years have taken me deeper into the realities spoken of here and I dare say if I delayed another six years there would be more still.

This text comes from a place deep inside of me and follows the journey of my heart in seeking to know the fullness of God in all that He is. I thank the brave souls who have travelled with me and encouraged me. I also acknowledge those who have given me the courage to believe that what I 'see' is theologically and doctrinally sound.

I want to acknowledge also the writings of C.S. Lewis, Brennan Manning, Henri J.M. Nouwen, Katharine Bushnell, Paul Tournier, and Madame Guyon (among others) whose writings have been a major influence in my spiritual growth and development.

I am so grateful for the wonderful privilege of having seen at close hand the love and walk of Jack and Dorothy Winter. Not enough can be said of how this couple set me on this path of discovery. Dorothy was the first woman I met who had true strength with dignity and humility, who showed me it was a good thing to look a little deeper than what was taken for granted in the Christianity of the day, especially in challenging the beliefs of those days concerning the role of woman. Jack and Dorothy were the first ones to let us truly see that the Christian life is simply learning to live a life of loving God and loving people.

I am also thankful for the life and ministry of Clay and Mary McLean (www.mcleanministries.org). Although I have only briefly met them once, I have listened extensively to Clay's teachings on the 'masculine and feminine' and its influence on broken sexuality. His work has been a significant influence on my own.

This book has not been written in isolation nor is this the first attempt. There has been a gracious coming together of gifted and insightful people to bring it to pass. Firstly, I want to thank Briar Whitehead for believing so deeply in this project and me, and for the work she has put toward it.

The manuscript of this book has gone through a number of phases and in the end has been brought together by the competence, patience and perseverance of my friend and co-worker Stephen Hill. Stephen has worked with notes, lecture transcripts, recordings and interviews to prepare this work for publication.

Finally I thank my best friend and husband James for all the encouragement he has given me over the years we have walked together.

Denise Jordan

Taupo, 2013

Foreword

This book is the product of many years of walking with God and of being involved with people who have extreme levels of personal brokenness.

Since early childhood through to her adult life, Denise has been exposed to much personal suffering as well as being a champion of those who endure suffering – from cleaning and bandaging the bleeding, beaten drunkard down the street as a child, to years of counselling those who are deeply sexually broken and the psychologically confused.

As long as I have known her, Denise has embodied the 'God chaser'. She is always seeking greater levels of the reality of God that will truly heal the broken-hearted. I know this, as I have been her husband and companion in her journey for the last forty-two years. During those years there were many times when she spoke into my life causing me to wonder if perhaps (for me at least) the Holy Spirit has another name – Denise. I can truly say that she has done me nothing but good all the years we have been together.

Denise has discovered that God our Father transcends gender and all that the human person is, came from Him. Therefore all that masculinity is and all that femininity is came from Him. The repercussions, consequences and ramifications of that fact alone will cause seismic shifts in the theology of many people.

I am sometimes amused by the attitudes of some people concerning women in ministry. We must remember that the first time anyone taught a Christian truth – it was taught by a woman. The resurrection of Jesus was first proclaimed by a woman and when the male disciples didn't receive it from her, Jesus Himself upbraided them. I have personally benefitted equally from the women as from the men who have ministered into my life over the years and at the head of that list is Denise.

I am confident that this book, being an expression of much that she has been directly taught by God, and gleaned from the deepest and richest writers of Christendom, will truly benefit all who read it. As you read this, open your heart and mind and submit to God's teaching, and it is my hope and belief that you will make a revolutionary leap in your walk with God.

M. James Jordan

1 | A Theology of the Heart

an interview with Denise Jordan

In working with Denise to bring this manuscript together, I wondered how the reader could be given access to the deep realities and issues that this book addresses. A preface or an explanatory chapter at the beginning may well have sufficed, however, the best way to introduce this book is to introduce readers to the author herself. So that is what we did. We began our dialogue with a few chosen questions but then found that the Spirit quickly enlivened our conversation together, bringing out something that is, I believe, full of vitality and insight. I honour Denise for opening her heart in such a way that makes reading the book a rich and rewarding experience. Stephen Hill.

Stephen Hill. *First of all, Denise, can I ask you what is in your heart in writing this book*

Denise Jordan. It's really because of some of my own life issues and some of the things that I have struggled with over the years. There are things that did not make sense to me for so long when I was growing up. Even when I got saved and was in a really good church there was still something inside me that didn't feel right, particularly when I was looking at my identity as a daughter. I could see how it could work for men. The Bible is full of references to brothers, sons, etc.; the vast majority of the Scriptures seemed to be in reference to the masculine and of course God is revealed in the Scriptures as Father. The deep question within me was, "What about women?" You see, I could observe in the life and ministry of

Jesus that He had a radically different perspective and a very different way in which He related to women than anyone else did. I could see that – because Jesus is the Son of God and perfectly revealed the Father – God *did* have a different way of seeing women to how it had always been portrayed, even through my understanding of the Bible.

Obviously you have pioneered this teaching both through who you are in yourself and also through speaking. You are taking a step beyond the current format of the ministry that you and James are involved in – speaking through schools and conferences – and now you want to release this on the printed page. What has changed that you now have a specific desire to put this into print?

It really comes down to this. For years, I have spoken about the mother heart of God and about the war that is being waged by the enemy against femininity for a very specific reason, that is, to destroy the image of God. When I have taught these things in conferences, seminars and schools the inevitable question always comes, "Is this in a book somewhere?" My answer to that question always has to be, "No," because the perspective that I teach and the way that I present it, to my knowledge, is not done anywhere else. There are books that are written about women's place in the church and arguing the point that women should be allowed to speak in the church, but I am really not interested in that argument.

Why not?

Because, to me, the real issues are much more fundamental than merely whether women should be allowed to speak in church. That is a side issue.

You are going to a much deeper level and dealing with much deeper root issues. You are attempting to answer a question that is much more foundational than an argument about the rights of women within churches.

Exactly! My personal opinion is this – I don't think we can even begin to address that particular issue until we come to the fuller understanding that God is both masculine and feminine and that we are created fully in His image as male and female. In some ways we are pioneering a new theological perspective here.

One thing that I would like you to address is this. Some might say that everything is in the written Word – the Logos. How does that fit in with the idea of 'pioneering' theology? Can you comment on this because it is also true that one of the very clearly stated values of Father-heart Ministries is that everything taught is to be based on Scripture? Can you say something about what you teach, for example, the mother heart of God in relation to being 'biblically based'?

One thing that James does is this – he holds up the Bible and says, "There is more in this book than has ever come out of this book!" That is so true. Everything that we teach is grounded solidly in the Scriptures. Everything that is new needs to be verified by three or four other Scriptures. Everything we teach on the mother heart of God or on masculinity and femininity as being the full image of God, for example, is grounded by at least three of four specific biblical passages. I say that, but to me, of course, the whole Bible is full of it. Once you begin to see it, you see it everywhere. There are very biblical reasons for saying what we say. We never speak anything new unless it can be fully grounded in the Scriptures. But, as you say, theology is a living thing. It is when it is not a living and developing thing that it becomes legalistic and dead. I believe we have come to a time in history when God is bringing this particular revelation forth. He is revealing more of Himself and giving us new insight and fresh understanding because of what is happening in the world. God has waited for a time when there is a clear need for this revelation and He is releasing it. There is a real need right now to know these things that we are teaching.

This is really a prophetic theology from the heart and to the heart of those who receive it.

Definitely – yes. Theology doesn't come out of objective study. Theology comes from your heart. It is a living thing. Your interpretation of Scripture comes from your heart. You will even hear God speak to you according to the state of your heart.

Yes, theology itself is a growing, living entity. If it is a true theology that comes from the heart and from God Himself it is, in that sense, constantly being created.

God is constantly revealing more of Himself to us. His word is "new every morning!" The Scripture says that He does not change, but He is new to us as He reveals more of Himself to us.

So the theological reactions to the teaching most likely come from the state of people's hearts and established belief systems?

I really believe that. When we are teaching on the mother heart of God we are touching emotions that are extremely deep. It takes courage to embrace something that may be very new when you are experiencing a lot of pain. One defence is to declare the theology to be flawed. When we are teaching this we are also countering a dominant theology that has been very much underpinned by misogyny. We establish biblically that God is both masculine and feminine.

So your starting point is your insight into the image of God from the early chapters of Genesis, that humanity was created in the image of God – male and female He created them. That is essentially the starting point that you take. You see 'the image' and from that you go back into the reality of the nature of God as containing masculine and feminine. Is that true?

Absolutely. That is really how this has come about. It is important for authentic theology to have its roots in Genesis – the book of beginnings. The notion of the full image of God being both male and female is established right at the beginning of the first book of the Bible. Having said that, however, something else was going on in my heart at the time. Around 1980, I was going through a time of deep healing in my own life and, because of some of my own life experiences I was finding it very difficult to become close and intimate with God as a 'male'. I was seeing it like that because of my own experiences, which had been very painful and negative. I was having great difficulty in fully opening my heart to God as father. I believe that many women have this problem, understandably so – because of being deeply hurt and damaged. Even some of the wording in Scripture can isolate women who are carrying misunderstanding and rejection. It is very scary for women who have been abused to open their hearts to what seems to be a 'male' God. That is where I was at. I was crying out to God and saying, "I wish You were like a mother! Then I could come close and be able to trust You."

This actually deals with the issue of the heart. Many people have difficulties seeing God as both masculine and feminine because of an overly cerebral approach to understanding. But it is about the heart. What you are saying is that the pain and need in your heart became the gateway to receiving this revelation of the mother heart of God.

Yes, God meets us where we are at. He sees the condition of our hearts. Theological understanding itself cannot heal the pain in our hearts.

Did you get this before you began to see the truth of 'the image' as both masculine and feminine? Was the initial catalyst, if you like, the need for the mothering love of God?

Yes. It was the cry for the comforting and nurturing love of God. It was the search for *anything at all* in God that is tender, nurturing and comforting, that which is essentially feminine. That was what really set me on this quest. But it wasn't for another ten years that God began to show me what was conveyed in the understanding of 'the image' – that He is indeed equally mother as He is father in the way that He relates to us in our hearts.

So you started on a quest of the heart that led you back to the Source of His image – revealing who He really is.

Yes, that is a good description of it.

Are you deliberate about the order in which you present the subjects?

Generally when I teach I begin with teaching about the image of God. I establish that God is both masculine and feminine. That leads me into teaching about misogyny. Then I finish off with the mother heart because I feel that many of the walls of resistance are broken down by that time – the resistance to God having a maternal heart.

What exactly is misogyny? Can you give a definition for it?

It simply means 'hatred of women' – I think it comes from the Greek.[1] I like to expand that definition, however, to be "the hatred of femininity" for reasons that will become clear in the book.

How impacting is the teaching on the Mother heart within Fatherheart Ministries' schools?

We find that teaching on the mother heart of God is a very significant key for helping some people open their hearts to receive the Father's love. When His love for us is just a masculine and dominant kind of love as has often been presented to us – it is virtually impossible to open your heart to be loved by a lawgiver and judge. But you can open your heart to be loved by a mother or by the One who comes to you as a loving Father unlike any earthly father. A lot of people have difficulty opening their hearts to a masculine figure when they have a predominant belief that God is solely masculine, as it were, and their impression of masculinity has been that which has been modelled through the world system and through fallenness, and through males in their own lives, sometimes including their own father. I am talking on a heart-level here, dealing with people's experiences, not their theological belief system. To understand that at the depths of God's heart is the heart that most of us would attribute to a tender and compassionate mother is a real help in opening our hearts to the Father. Many times we find that is when we get the breakthrough and by that time we have already laid a lot of the foundation in the revelation of God as Father.

---

1   Greek, *Misogunia* "woman hater" from *miso* for 'hate' and *gyne* meaning 'woman'.

The 'mother issue' is very primordial, isn't it?

Certainly. The issue of comfort (which God uses in the feminine language of Isaiah 66:13) is so foundational because we begin our lives humanly in the womb of our mother. Fathers may be present or absent but we start life within the womb. There is no getting away from that. The deficit of mothering love and comfort needs to be addressed before the fathering can come in.

It seems that the issue of comfort is one of the major needs today – both for Christians and non-Christians alike.

Yes. Actually, when I first spoke on the mother heart of God and Jack Winter first heard me put this into words, his comment was, "Maybe what we have been calling this ministry of the Father's love has been a ministry of His mother's love." Jack had been ministering love and comfort for many years and had even talked about God having a mothering love but had never put it into words as we have. It is primarily a mother who brings comfort to the children. The mandate of our ministry has, in one sense, increased since Jack Winter made that statement but I still feel that it was significant.

We could say this is a prophetic message. What does it mean to you to be 'prophetic'?

I wouldn't want to call myself 'prophetic' or claim that it is prophetic, but what I would say is this; someone has said, "the head has knowledge that the heart doesn't have and the heart has knowledge that the head doesn't have."[2] I believe that this book is bringing out truths and realities that are known primarily to the heart. The heart will resonate with

---

2 This could be a reference to Blaise Pascal's maxim, "The heart has its reasons which reason does not understand."

the truth of what I am saying. The hearts of many people believe this but their minds are telling them that these realities are actually too good to be true or their theology has no room for it. So to say it again – I don't think of it so much as being 'prophetic' as being 'heart-knowledge'.

So, just to be clear, it is more a knowledge of the heart rather than being specifically prophetic in the way that we have understood 'prophetic'.

The word 'prophetic' has been so overused in the last twenty years, hasn't it? It has been so overused that I personally want to get away from that particular word.

Is it a stretch to place femininity within the very heart and essence of the Godhead?

We talk about God birthing things. God has birthed creation. To physically birth something you need femininity. If we talk about the spirit as being the very deepest part of who we are – the Scripture says that God is spirit and the word for 'spirit' in Hebrew is in the feminine gender. The attributes of that are seen in Galatians – the fruits of the Spirit are what you would generally see as being traits of the feminine. It is His heart that we come to Him by our spirit connecting with His Spirit.

C.S. Lewis said that God is so masculine that we are all feminine before Him, (or something to that effect). That may appear to contradict what you are saying. Can you try and express why those two paradigms are true?

In my opinion, C.S. Lewis makes that statement for one reason – because only God has the power to initiate. He is the initiator and it is that one aspect above all others that makes Him masculine. But if you look at God's desire for intimate relationship, that is truly feminine. We are feminine before

Him because we can only respond to His initiative but His desire to have deep heart-to-heart intimacy with us is what we would define as a feminine characteristic.

> *Will this understanding bring a new sense of freedom to people? What does it do to the human heart to see God in terms of His femininity?*

I really believe that when we know we are loved and when we experience love – that is what makes us completely human. And when we are completely human we are fully alive – living life, enjoying life, enjoying relationships. I think it is indisputable that the masses of humanity in this world are looking for love. Everything that people get into – the typical addictions but also addiction to things like work or shopping – is all to mask that deep need to feel loved and lovable. The desire and need that we have to be loved is what God has already put there so that He can fulfill it.

As long as we see Him through the old paradigm that is limited to the characteristics of the 'fallen masculine' this will never happen. That is why the whole understanding of misogyny is so important because there is a mastermind who is operating to keep us from ever knowing who God really is.

> *So you would say that the deep need of our hearts is like a mirror that reflects back into the nature of God Himself. If I desperately need the comfort of a mother's love, for example, that cannot possibly be in my heart if there isn't an answer to it within the Godhead itself.*

That is exactly what I mean. We can only need something and long for something that is initially in God Himself and that can only be fulfilled through Him.

> *This takes me back to a theological term called 'an-thropomorphism' which means that we project human*

characteristics onto God to help us understand Him. However, there is another term called 'theomorphism' that says that all human characteristics (obviously not those which are fallen) are reflections of what is already in God.

Absolutely.

So, in that sense, everything in humanity that is not fallen is in the image of what is in the Godhead already.

I totally believe that. I couldn't see it any other way. Peter Kreeft in his book, *Heaven: The Heart's Deepest Longing*, quotes C.S. Lewis saying something like, "Sometimes I think that we don't think enough about heaven. Other times I don't think we think of anything else" [3] The whole premise of the book is that our heart is created for heaven. He asks, for example, why do we seek perfection when we have never seen perfection? But we go on seeking it because there is something in our heart that says it exists. His whole book is a beautifully written apologetic. I believe that the things we long for and never receive are there as (to use Peter Kreeft's term) 'heavenly hauntings.' I love that term – they are hauntings from heaven. Peter Kreeft uses the example (among others) of romantic love. Romantic love is so elusive – you pursue it and you may get a fleeting satisfaction from it but that is actually a haunting from heaven. All of a sudden our heart sees something and we run after it, but what we are really seeking is heaven, it is that experience of living in God.

Can you tell me what writers have influenced you most in terms of your heart-theology and your teaching?

3   "There have been times when I think we do not desire heaven but more often I find myself wondering whether, in our heart of hearts, we have ever desired anything else" as quoted by Peter Kreeft in *Heaven: The Heart's Deepest Longing (Expanded Edition)* (Ignatius Press, 1989).

Firstly, I would have to say the late Brennan Manning because he was a man who was very in touch with his own brokenness and yet still had the grace to have faith towards God, and because of that he found a God who was completely loving and nurturing, a God who would always give that one more chance for restoration. In that, Brennan Manning came to a deep knowledge and understanding of the heart of God. When he wrote, his words were full of grace giving so much hope to people.

I would also say that one of my major influences has been the work of C.S. Lewis. I believe he was a man who really saw heaven. He came from a place of incredible loneliness and rejection as a young boy but he found a place in God Himself. His writings really take me to another level and open my eyes to another dimension.

Another writer is Henri Nouwen whose work I love for similar reasons as that of Brennan Manning.

A writer that I really like is Peter Kreeft. Part of his life's work is to write about and explain the thought of C.S. Lewis. I have taken a lot from him.

In terms of counselling, emotional healing etc. I have read a lot of Paul Tournier, who again was a man who had lost a lot in life but who really sought God to meet his needs and who had tremendous grace and compassion for people. His writings are very insightful and completely free of judgement. He understood the human condition with a lot of compassion.

Also, Leanne Payne who I have read a lot of, particularly when I was involved with Living Waters. She has written on a deep level about masculinity and femininity and draws a lot from the writings of C.S. Lewis.

A huge influence in the development of my spirituality was the writings of Madame Guyon. She was a woman who was living in an extremely difficult situation. She was persecuted by her husband, suffered the deaths of children, experienced rejection and imprisonment. She suffered an amazing amount of grief in her life, but she overcame it by going deeper and deeper into God. She had a whole theology of suffering. Her whole life and message was about the comfort that could be found in Jesus.

> *When did you get a revelation and experience of God's mothering love? I'm trying to get a sense of timing here in relation to your life and ministry*

I think I began to see it theologically before I really had the experience of Him loving me as a mother, that real nurturing, comforting love.

> *A lot of these things are not immediately obvious when you pick up the Bible and read it. That is why so many people think in particular ways about God, but yet when you experienced this awesome love of God you began to see things in a completely different light. You had a radically new theology, in that sense. Sometimes I wonder why it isn't more plainly spoken in the written text. Have you anything to say about that?*

There is the reference about "a God who hides Himself," a God who loves to be sought out by those who seek Him. He has built something into us that loves to search things out and that loves mystery. That is part of it.

The other thing is this. We talk a lot in this ministry about the two trees – the tree of life and the tree of the knowledge of good and evil. The tree of the knowledge of good and evil is like when Jesus said to the Pharisees in John 5:39, "You search the Scriptures because you think that in them you will find eternal life, but they testify of Me." You don't find this in Scripture *unless* you are eating from the right tree!

When you are eating from the tree of life – from that place of love, from that experience of being loved – you get deeper revelations.

I understand now what Jesus meant when He said that there were many things He would have liked to tell His disciples but He couldn't do so because they couldn't bear them. I believe that if He had said them then that they may well have sounded heretical to those in a culture of Law. But, you see, love sees things differently. Paul said, of his experience in the third heaven, how he heard things which were "not lawful for man to utter." That could be read that he wasn't allowed to talk about them, but I believe it also refers to the content of what was spoken – that it was way beyond 'the law' – they would sound wrong to the religious mind.

> *Didn't Paul say, "All things are lawful but not all are profitable to me." (1Co 6:12) and, "To the pure all things are pure?" (Tit 1:15). Those are actually very sweeping and shocking statements, if you think about it! He was talking about something beyond the knowledge of good and evil. The tree of knowledge puts very clear definitions and boundaries in place but in the tree of life the only criteria is love and how love impacts on the other.*

The tree of life sheds an entirely different light on everything. I wish I always saw the Scriptures through that lens, but that is my hope. Sometimes I come back to eating from the tree of life and think, "Now I see" – I see the *real* meaning of the Scripture. We cannot really preach this yet because we (the body of Christ) are not ready to hear it.

> *What can you communicate? What can you preach? What can you write about? What is the entry point to this?*

Even when I speak I don't want to go beyond the hearers. I want those who read this book to be able to understand and receive what I am trying to communicate with God's help. If I don't communicate with people where they are at, I rob them of the good that is in this book. One thing that I learned from someone who was very influential in our lives was that he spoke into where we were at but there was a depth in him that somehow conveyed the sense of there being a lot more that he wasn't saying. It gave me a hunger. I was thinking, "I want to know what he knows. He's not telling us everything. What is he *not* saying?" That's how I want to communicate. I want to create a hunger in people so that they search for themselves.

Have you any concerns that criticism might be levelled at what you say, or that it might be detracted from?

No, I don't have any concerns about that because I believe there is always unfolding revelation. As we said earlier, theology is a living thing. If it isn't, it is just dead religion.

Also, what I have observed over the years is that some people agree with one person's theology and don't agree with the next. There are many schools of theology and many perspectives and all can be scripturally based and scripturally proven – as can this! This teaching is not something that is way out there. It can be soundly and solidly verified in Scripture. Personally, I feel very comfortable in my own spirit about it, but Scripture also underpins it.

Finally, Denise, what are you hoping that this book will achieve? What impact do you want it to have?

One of my concerns is the ways that we have seen God and consequently the way that we have related to Him. If you look at the 'fallen masculine' and the 'fallen feminine' – we have tended to see God very much in terms of the 'fallen masculine' – angry, controlling, unfeeling, cruel, judgmental, dominating, etc. – someone who punishes every little thing that you do wrong. That has been one of the problems with seeing God as purely masculine – and we haven't even seen Him in the good sense of the true masculine. Historical Christianity and indeed many of the great theologians that have shaped our belief system (whether we are aware of it or not) have seen God from a fallen perspective. We have seen Him through the paradigm of our own fallenness. I want people to really know His tenderness and compassion. The Bible is crammed full of these words but they are so hidden because of our prejudiced thinking and because of the way that we see Him from this distorted overly masculine perspective. My journey has been my own longing to encounter a God who would never abandon me, who wouldn't condemn me and I want people to see that reality. For many of us, when the chips are down, it is our *mother* who stands with us. My feeling is that if we know that God is also a mother (in that sense) to us, we could then be a lot more secure in our relationship with Him. This is my hope.

2 | The Restoration of the Image of God

But he had never till now seen the reality. For now he saw this living Paradise, the Lord and the Lady, as the resolution of discords, the bridge that spans what would else be a chasm in creation, the keystone of the whole arch. C.S. Lewis

Tis Love unites what sin divides:
The centre where all bliss resides… Madame Guyon

When I look back at the things that God has taught James and me (the things from which our lives and ministry flow), I have found that He has taken us time and time again to Genesis, the 'book of beginnings.' He has taken us back to those first chapters, to the account of the creation, to the Fall and what happened to our forefathers in the Garden. We have come to believe with all our hearts that it is the Father's intention to bring to every person a restoration to that quality of life and relationship, which humanity enjoyed with God in the Garden in the very beginning. That would be a good start, wouldn't it? But that may only be the beginning! I believe that the purposes of God actually extend beyond restoring that which was lost through the Fall.

When James and I came into a fuller understanding of what the 'image of God' means we found it to be invaluable in terms of giving us a perspective of life as God originally intended it to be. To gain an understanding of what it means to be created in God's image brings a richer and more whole perspective from which we can see ourselves as human beings, a perspective of our relationship to God and His eternal purposes for our relationship with Him.

In Genesis 1:26-28 we read:

Then God said, "Let us make man in our image, in our likeness, and let them rule over the fish of the sea and the birds of the air, over the livestock, over all the earth, and over all the creatures that move along the ground." So God created man in His own image, in the image of God He created him; male and female He created them.

These verses, of course, are very well known. Familiar as they are, a huge amount of meaning is contained within them. At the outset, it is very important to understand that the Hebrew word 'man' here in verse 26 is a generic term *adam* meaning 'mankind' and is inclusive of both man and woman. This verse speaks of the intention of God prior to the act of creating, and His intention was to create mankind of both male and female.

We see clearly from this segment of the narrative that God wanted to create an image of Himself – something to reflect accurately within its environment the nature and personality of the Creator. We also see that when God wanted to create an image of Himself, He created male and female. In other words, it takes a man *and* a woman to fully display what the image of God is like. Contrary to a lot of the prevailing theology and cultural norms throughout history, the image of God is not only a masculine image or confined to the male. God's image is displayed in *both* male and female.

The other crucial thing to understand here is that the commission to rule was not only given to the (male) man as such. Nor was it given solely to the woman. The commission and authority to rule, rather, was given to *the image*. God gave the mandate to rule to male and female together. Another good reason for going back to the early chapters of Genesis is what is known as 'the law of first mention'. This is a theological principle whereby a doctrinal precedent is set by going back to its initial mention in the biblical text. The closer to the beginning that we see something the more authority it has. Therefore we see God's intention very clearly enunciated in the book of Genesis. In the very first chapter of the first book we see that God has given authority to His image, thus setting a precedent. Sadly, this has been obscured by many centuries of misogyny (the hatred of women and femininity) – but increasingly we see God reversing this trend by bringing revelation to expose the lies of the enemy.

In making these opening and foundational statements there is another very important factor that underlies what I am saying. When I use the terms 'male' and 'female' I am not speaking primarily in terms of biological and sexual characteristics. Masculinity and femininity run much deeper than, and extend beyond, the issue of biology. This will become clearer as you read through this chapter. The point I wish to make is that 'masculinity' and 'femininity' is a greater reality of which male and female sexuality is only, as it were, a part. In the words of C.S. Lewis, "Gender is a reality, and a more fundamental reality than sex."[1] There is a greater

---

1   C.S. Lewis continues in this passage from *Perelandra*, Reprint Edition (HarperCollins Publishers, 2005), "Sex is, in fact, merely the organic adaptation to organic life of a fundamental polarity which divides all created beings. Female sex is simply one of the things that have feminine gender; there are many others, and Masculine and Feminine meet us on planes of reality where male and female would be simply meaningless. Masculine is not attenuated male, nor feminine attenuated female. On the contrary, the male and female

reality of God that is expressed in us that our physical characteristics. This is a reality that is expressed in all of us – in body, soul, and spirit. God's image can thus be more accurately described in terms of 'masculinity' and 'femininity.'

Within each of us is contained both God's masculinity and God's femininity – and that is what makes us in His likeness. What makes us human is to have both masculinity and femininity contained within a body. Generally, the female sex would contain more of God's femininity and the male sex would contain more of God's masculinity. However, I want to stay away from being too traditional or stereotypical in my statements. The balance of masculinity and femininity within each person is not easily defined or pigeonholed. Every person is created by God with his or her unique balance of masculinity and femininity. To attempt to give too tight a definition of what a man or a woman should be like can take away from appreciating the uniqueness of how God has created each of His individual children.[2] That is all I will say at this point, as everything will become clearer as you continue reading.

Regardless of whether we are male or female, God has put His masculinity and His femininity within each one of us. When God expresses who He is in creation, He does so by creating a man and a woman, thus expressing both His

---

of organic creatures are rather faint and blurred reflections of masculine and feminine. Their reproductive functions, their differences in strength and size, partly exhibit, but partly also confuse and misrepresent, the real polarity." p.253. There is a substantial section devoted to this idea of the masculine and feminine in this part of the book.

2   The famous Swiss physician and author, Dr Paul Tournier comments, " ... it is understood that there is masculine and feminine in every human being, whether man or woman. There are men who have this sense of the person, and women whose bent is towards technology and things. The complementarity of the sexes is not only an external matter between men and women, but also internal, between the two tendencies which are present in each of us." From *The Gift of Feeling,* (John Knox Press, 1979).

masculinity and His femininity. Let me reiterate; God is not just masculine. He is masculine *and* feminine. God may be referred to generally as "He" – but this is not primarily because of His gender. It is true also, that Jesus was a man, but the point I am making here is that both masculinity and femininity are characteristics of the Godhead, and Genesis makes this very clear.

It would not be accurate to assert either, that God is without gender, that He is a 'genderless being', so to speak. God is spirit – true – but it is clear from this passage in Genesis that masculinity and femininity are to be found in the substance of who God is. Rather than speaking of God as being *without* gender, it would be more fitting to say that God transcends gender. In fact, He contains *all* of the traits of masculinity and of femininity within His divine nature.

To help us with this, it is important to realise that there is nothing that God created in mankind that was not in His image. Consider that for a while. When God created the man and the woman before the Fall, was there anything in them that was not in His image? No! Prior to being deceived by the serpent and driven from the Garden, there was nothing *within* the man or the woman that was not an expression of God's image. He was fully intentional in giving the commission to rule the earth to His image – both masculine and feminine. Contrary to what many believe, it wasn't only the man who was mandated to rule the earth and exercise dominion. Both man and woman were appointed to have dominion in a synergy of the authority of love over the created order. Many theologians and denominations have failed to see in the Scriptures that women have the right to rule alongside men. This passage in Genesis very clearly and specifically addresses this misconception and exposes it as fundamentally flawed.

What are the unique characteristics of masculinity and femininity? If we can have some insight into what these are we can gain, to some extent, an understanding of what the image of God is like. Before the Fall we have a perfect model of what man and woman were intended to be in the creative purposes of God. If we look at the image then we can project back from that, as it were, to see the *reality* of the nature of God. When looking at these traits of masculinity and femininity I am focusing on the fact that these are supremely and originally in the nature of God. Remember also that all of us as individuals have a unique mix of masculinity and femininity within us, so many of us will recognise traits of both masculinity and femininity in our behaviour and way of relating.

Masculine characteristics in the Godhead

- ¤ Masculinity could be described as the *'doing'* side of God's nature. It is the active aspect of God. It is about 'going forth'. "The Lord will go forth like a warrior" (Isa 42:13 NASB). When women 'do' or 'go forth,' etc., they do so out of masculinity within them.

- ¤ Masculinity wants to *'know about'* something – to gain information. Men generally are more interested in the size of the engine in a car, for example, or the memory capacity of a computer.

- ¤ Masculinity has the power to *initiate.* Women also initiate but they do this out of their masculine side. C.S. Lewis has said that God Himself is so masculine that the whole creation is feminine before Him. This is because God is the great initiator and that, according to C.S. Lewis, is what makes Him masculine. He is the Original Source. Our life, our existence, our salvation and redemption – everything is initiated by Him.

- Masculinity has the power to *defend*. Masculinity has the power to stand for what is true, for what is just. It has the power to withhold the onslaught of the enemy against that which it believes in and holds dear.

- Masculinity is '*the protector*'. It has the power to rescue. This is similar to the previous point. We see this in the young boy David who protected his flock from lions and bears (1Sa 17:34-37).

- Masculinity has the ability to *give form* to things. It is able to bring order where there is chaos.

- Masculinity *prevails* in face of adversity. We see this supremely in Jesus who "endured the cross" and "endured such opposition from sinful men" (Heb 12:2).

- Masculinity has *honesty* and *integrity*. Masculinity is very connected with *truth* and standing for what is true. Masculinity has power to speak and stand for truth.

- Masculinity has the power to *complete* and to *finish* what it has begun. We see this in the life of Jesus, that He completed the work that the Father had given Him to do (Joh 17:4). Paul the apostle said, "I have fought the good fight, I have finished the race, I have kept the faith" 2Ti 4:7).

- Masculinity has the power to be *committed*. In Luke 9:51 some versions say that Jesus set his face *like flint* to go to Jerusalem.

- Masculinity relates to the '*head*' whereas femininity relates to the heart, and both are essential to sustain life.

- Masculine ways of learning and knowing are different from feminine ways of knowing. Typical masculine ways of knowing are *rational, observable, logical* and *linear*. Masculinity likes to be able to definitively prove a thesis by observation, collection of data/evidence and by testing.

I always think of masculinity as being like a straight line. It is strong, focused and it is 'out there'. It goes 'beyond'.

Feminine characteristics in the Godhead

◻ Femininity is the *'being'* side of God's nature. God is at rest and able to just 'be'. Psalm 46:10 says, "Be still and know that I am God." Femininity is at rest and content within itself. Out of this it has the power to bring rest to others. King David said, "…You made me trust in You at my mother's breast" (Psa 22:9).

◻ Femininity has the ability to *receive and respond.* This is possibly the principal characteristic of femininity. Men do operate in this otherwise they would never be able to receive anything from God. This, however, is much more profound in women. The very essence of femininity is in the ability to receive. A woman receives the seed that has the potential for a child to grow. There is something in women that is able to receive and respond in ways that men cannot.

◻ Femininity has the desire to *know and be known in relationship.* This is very different from the masculine, which desires to 'know about' something or observe something. You can see this exemplified in a typical interaction between a husband and a wife at the end of the day. Generally speaking, men will usually give the minimum of factual information. Women, however, desire to know the emotions behind the facts. Often men are reluctant to ask a woman how her day has been, because she responds with 'too much information'! The masculine imparts information and facts – the feminine is more empathetic – seeing the perspective of the other.

¤ Femininity seeks *union and connection outside of oneself.* I can see the heart of God revealed in these characteristics. His greatest desire is to know and to be known in relationship. The whole Bible is written to this end – that we might know Him and that He would be revealed to us. There is a tremendous desire in the heart of God for mutual knowing. In the human body both head and heart are absolutely indispensable. You cannot live without either of them. You cannot say that one is more vital than the other but they have different functions.

¤ Femininity *imparts life* to others. Children feed from the mother's nutrients. We have noticed that when people in ministry speak or preach from the heart, and not just from the head, they will impart life to others. Life is imparted when a speaker speaks from a feminine understanding – with gentleness, empathy and compassion. It is more than just being cerebral, using only logic and knowledge. The life of the Spirit can flow when they speak from the heart. Men who are locked into their masculinity, having rendered inoperative their femininity, generally just give information but don't impart life. People who impart life in preaching have an operative feminine component. Because this desires union in relationship it makes a living connection with the hearer.

¤ Femininity *comforts* in a different way than masculinity. God says very intentionally, "As a *mother* comforts her child, so I will comfort you" (Isa 6:13). The comfort of a mother is a comfort that surrounds and succours whereas a father enables the little one to get back up and return to the fray. We see that if a child falls and grazes their little knee, for example, the initial instinct will generally be to run past the father and into the mother's arms to receive her unique motherly comfort.

◻ Femininity has the ability and power to *nurture*. This is closely connected with the imparting of life. This is very clearly seen in breastfeeding the newborn child, for example, sustaining the new life outside the womb with her own body. Nurturing sustains life. A father will desire to provide for the life of the child but a mother will desire to nurture and enrich the life of the child – to enhance life. Obviously, as the child grows and develops the father will enhance its life as well.

◻ Femininity is characterised by *creativity* and *wisdom*. In fact, wisdom is personified in Scripture as being feminine. (Pro 8:1-3).

◻ Typical feminine ways of learning and knowing are *discerning* and *intuitive* – very different from masculine ways of knowing. Often women can have intuitions in relationships. For example, there may be something about a person that they just do not trust. They cannot explain it. It is just a feminine intuition that is communicating this hesitancy to trust that particular person. The capacity to receive revelation is a feminine trait, both in men and women.

◻ Femininity gives a sense of *belonging*. In contrast to masculinity (which is a straight line – going forth, pushing forward and conquering), femininity is more like a circle. Femininity is a circle of life which encloses within its circumference, relationships, comfort, creativity, wisdom, nurturing, and much more. If masculinity is about 'the head', then femininity is about 'the heart'. Both of these are of equal value and importance and are equally indispensable for life.

These are by no means complete lists, but they do give us some help in understanding the characteristics of masculinity and femininity as originating within the Godhead. When we read these lists we see more clearly that both masculinity and femininity need to be operative within us as they were in Jesus. Often, because the heart is not valued, men will tend to repress their heart and live from 'the head'. Many men are told from the time they are little boys that it is 'girly' to show emotions. As a result, it is a trait of masculinity to live from the mind and be overly cerebral. Often men will have their heart subdued because their God-given femininity has been suppressed. Many men have no language at all to give adequate expression to how they feel about anything. When the suppressed femininity is set free there is a restored connection to the heart. We see in King David a wonderful example of a man who was strongly operative in both his masculinity and his femininity.

You could sum this all up by putting it like this: God's intention for the Masculine is to be *Authority with Nurturing*; His intention for the Feminine is to be *Nurturing with Authority*.[3]

Jesus is the complete example of this. But, for me, a woman, to become like Jesus does not make me more masculine. For a man to become like Jesus does not mean a repressing or denying of his masculinity. There is strength and dignity in masculinity and in femininity. The woman in Proverbs 31:25, "...is clothed with strength and dignity." This passage is a wonderful example of how true femininity is meant to be. Also, in reading the Song of Solomon we can find many examples of the traits of true femininity and true masculinity as the two lovers relate to one another.

I have outlined some of the traits of masculinity and femininity that are, first and foremost, displayed in the Godhead. Needless to say, it is not a complete picture, but it

---

3 Attributed to Clay McLean.

does go some way to helping us understand this truth. To put it simply, masculinity is to be likened to a straight line – going forth, giving definition, and delineating. Femininity, on the other hand, is more like a circle – encompassing, enveloping, surrounding and comforting. These depictions give us some idea of the essence of masculinity and femininity within the nature and character of God.

I cannot put it better than C.S. Lewis who describes the essence of masculinity thus:

> ...[Masculinity] seemed to have the look of one standing armed, at the ramparts of his own archaic world, in ceaseless vigilance, his eyes ever roaming the earthward horizon whence his danger came long ago...'a sailor's look ... eyes that are impregnated with distance.'"

In contrast, Lewis speaks of femininity:

> ...but the eyes of [femininity] opened, as it were, inward, as if they were the curtained gateway to a world of waves and murmurings and wandering airs, of life that rocked in winds and splashed on mossy stones and descended as the dew and arose sunward in a tin-spun delicacy of mists."[4]

I will now look at the third chapter of Genesis, which recounts the Fall of humanity. Note that God *did not* curse the man and the woman. Rather, He cursed the serpent, and He cursed the ground. However, in addressing the woman and the man, what He did do was give a description of what life would now be like for them outside of the garden in Eden. Many commentators and theologians have taken God's words in Genesis 3:16-19 as a direct curse upon the man and the woman. But these words are, I believe, to be understood as descriptive rather than prescriptive. In other words, they relate what the inevitable consequences of eating from the

---

4   C.S. Lewis, *Perelandra*, Reprint Edition (HarperCollins Publishers 2005).

Tree of Knowledge would be. Because sin has entered in they are both now cut off from the Source of life – the Father Himself – so there will be (in the words of Leanne Payne) a 'broken image' of what God is really like. Satan succeeded (temporarily, at least) in distorting the image of God as it was accurately reflected in the harmonious unity of the man and the woman. God's original intention to have Himself portrayed (in masculine and feminine attributes) through 'the image' was now disrupted because of the Fall.

In the opening verses of Genesis 5 it says, "When God created man (i.e., 'mankind') He made him in the likeness of God. He created them male and female; at the time they were created He blessed them and called them 'man.'" The word used here is the Hebrew word *adam*. Then it follows on to say, "When Adam had lived 130 years, he had a son in his own likeness, in his own image…" From this we see more evidence of the departure from the image of God. Mankind (*adam*) originally created as male and female in the image and likeness of God, brought forth this son, Seth, who was now in *their* image. Note that the shift here in the bearing of image and likeness. From now on it is 'like father, like son' (so to speak); Adam and Eve's child is an image of them in their fallen state, and no longer in God's image.[5]

God told the woman what the consequences of partaking of the tree of knowledge of good and evil would be, "I will greatly increase your pain in childbearing; with pain you will give birth to children. Your desire will be for your husband and he will rule over you." (Gen 3:16)

---

[5] It is interesting that the Scripture does not speak of Cain and Abel in these terms, but only Seth. Could it be that the 'image of God' did not cease immediately after their departure from the garden – but rather faded gradually? It gives food for thought.

What God is saying here is that – as a result of the Fall – the male gender would now be out of touch with His heart. Indeed, the man would also be out of touch with his own human heart. He would no longer be in connection with the Source. God had given them dominion, but God is telling the woman here that dominion over creation is lost only to be replaced with domination. Dominion can only be exercised from a heart of love and a heart of nurture. When the heart is disconnected, a self-centred domination replaces it. Domination is an issue of power; and it is not interested in the interests of others but only in self-interest and self-aggrandisement.

Dominion was given to the image because the feminine part of the image brings 'heart' into the equation. To take away the feminine is to take away the nurturing and loving heart and there cannot possibly be dominion. The masculine, cut off from its heart, rises up and begins to dominate. The dominion of love is replaced by a domination of control and power.

"Your desire will be for your husband" (Gen 3:16): the feminine trait of wanting to know and be known in relationship, to connect on a heart to heart level, will now be frustrated.

In all my years of counselling, what has stood out to me more than anything is a deep and primordial loneliness that has its roots in the Fall. It comes from the deep disconnection of the human heart from the heart of God, both in men and in women. In the past, I specifically taught on the subject of loneliness within our schools and conferences. However, I stopped doing this because I discovered that conferences and schools were an entirely inappropriate context for teaching on this issue. When a person really gets in touch with the depth of the loneliness within their heart, it is a pain that cannot be dealt with in a public setting. There is a huge chasm of loneliness within the heart of the human race and it comes from being disconnected to the Source. It comes from being cut off from the Father Himself. As a result, we are unable to connect heart to heart.

When God said to the woman that her desire would be for her husband, what He meant was that she would seek deep connection but he would be unable to connect on a heart level because of disconnection from the divine Source. The level that the woman really wants to relate on is now stifled and inaccessible because of the man's deep isolation from his heart. We have seen this a lot in marriages and relationships. Often the woman has the dilemma of wanting to connect deeply, but she expresses this in an unhealthy way. She tries to connect through her own fallenness instead of receiving her identity from the Father. We were intended from the very beginning to get our identity from the Father as His beloved sons and daughters. In contrast to this, fallen femininity tries to gain identity from relationships. Often a woman will identify herself solely on the basis of the relationships that she has, whether it be a boyfriend, a husband, friends or even her children. Fallen femininity seeks to gain identity – not from the Father – but from human relationships.

"He will rule over you." After the Fall, instead of having dominion based on co-equality man rose up in fallen masculinity and took domination. Sadly, Christendom has taken this statement, "He shall rule over you" as a divine edict. It has been interpreted as being a prescription rather than a description of what would inevitably happen. Many, from the Church Fathers through to contemporary theologians and church leaders, have misinterpreted these words as some sort of divine precedent that men are supposed to rule over women. But what God really meant (you could say, as a forewarning) was this: Now that the man has fallen and become a self-centred being rather than a being that is God-focused and other-centred – he will seek to exercise dominance over you.

The wonderful reality is that Jesus has countered this tendency and reversed this trend. The apostle Paul brings this out in Ephesians 5:25, when he admonishes:

> *Husbands, love your wives, just as Christ loved the Church and gave Himself up for her to make her holy, cleansing her with the washing of water through the word, and to present her to Himself as a radiant church, without stain or wrinkle or any other blemish, but holy and blameless. In this same way, husbands ought to love their wives as their own bodies. He who loves his wife loves himself. After all, no one ever hated his own body, but he feeds and cares for it, just as Christ does the Church...*

Jesus, as the 'second Adam' restored back the true and original blueprint of dominion. He demonstrated how the husband should love his wife by laying down his life for her and having the same attitude for her as Christ does for His church. Jesus had made this clear when the Pharisees tested Him on the issue of divorce, which was the subject of a fierce rabbinical debate in that day.[6] It seems they were pressing Him to take a particular viewpoint, however Jesus went back to the beginning and the original purposes of God:

> *Haven't you read,' He replied, 'that at the beginning the Creator made them male and female, and said, 'For this reason a man will leave his father and mother and be united to his wife, and the two will become one flesh'?*

---

6 Two leading rabbis of that time, Shammai and Hillel, founded two opposing schools of thought which had very differing opinions on divorce among other things. This was more than likely the context in which Jesus was questioned.

So they are no longer two, but one. Therefore what God has joined together let not man separate.

He went on to say that Moses allowed divorce in some circumstances, " ... *because your hearts were hard. But it was not this way from the beginning.*"[7] The hardening of the heart was the catalyst for a rupture of the original harmony that they enjoyed. Jesus, however, restored how it was 'in the beginning' – God's original template for human relationships.

Characteristics of Fallen Femininity

I have observed *four major ways* in which the Fallen Feminine manifests and expresses itself as a response to male domination.

¤ Firstly, she has risen up in the 'fallen masculine' and has become domineering and controlling. She has risen up and said, "You will *not* dominate me! In fact, I will dominate you!" You will get what I would call 'the strong woman' that everyone fears. She can be ruthless. She has lost touch with her femininity and now lives in the 'fallen masculine' dominating role.

¤ The second way that femininity has responded out of fallenness is to become extremely weak where she has none of the good masculine attributes at all. She cannot make decisions and is constantly dependent on others. She is weak in a very fallen way – you could say 'spineless.' Instead of being a giver of life she sucks the life out of those around her. Instead of having a life of her own, which overflows to others, she sucks the life out of her family or out of anyone that is around her. She uses terms like, "Poor me," or, "I cannot do this," or, "They won't give anything to me." She is a very disempowered

---

7   Mark 10:1-9.

being. This is also evident in men who may become extremely passive – the 'fallen feminine' in the man has taken precedence and dominance over any masculinity. This expression of fallenness has a very passive and non-responsive mentality – a victim complex. The masculine traits of decision-making, standing for truth, righteousness and 'the good' have been sublimated by perpetual defeatism and negativity. A biblical example that occurs to me is that of the man at the Pool of Bethesda in John 5:1-15. This man was trapped in his inability to get himself into the pool when the angel moved upon the waters. He seemed to be hindered by his own defeatism and negativity. "Sir, I have no one to help me into the pool when the water is stirred. While I am trying to get in, someone else goes down ahead of me." Jesus, tellingly, asked him the question, "Do you *want* to get well?" in a deliberate move to challenge his passive mindset. To be made whole you need to rise up in the good of the masculine – to make a decision, to look away from your problem and to be willing to respond in faith when the moment of opportunity comes to you. The 'fallen feminine' is the classic manipulator. Because of her powerlessness and lack of healthy masculinity, she has to resort to underhanded means and manipulation to get what she wants.

¤ The third way that I have observed is that of 'the seducer'. She manipulates also but she does so by seduction. Obviously, she seduces sexually but she does this as a way of dominating. She exerts power over men by seducing them. I have had a lot to do with women who have used this as a way to merely survive. In all my dealings with women like this I have rarely met one who actually respects men. This is self-hatred spilling over into hatred of men, seeking to prove to themselves that everyone (including themselves) is rotten to the core. No-one feels good about themselves in this scenario. You can see a very lucid description of this type of woman in Proverbs 7 and Proverbs 9:15-18.

¤ The fourth response to male domination that I have observed is where femininity has completely rejected men and all that is masculine. This is an extreme form of feminism that envisages an existence in which men have no place whatsoever. Often lesbianism can come out of such a response, when a woman has been so hurt by men that she chooses not to have them in her life at all – and so chooses a sexual partner of the same gender. If she wishes to have children she can do so by means of artificial insemination. We also see this response in intellectual circles, for example, where some radical feminist university professors have gone as far as banning male students from their lectures. This response extends to arguing *against* sexual equality and supporting the idea that women should govern men, without exception.

It goes without saying that there are nuances and complexities within these observations that I have made, however they do give a general indication of how the Fall has affected femininity as a response to the fallen masculine.

Characteristics of Fallen Masculinity

Fallen masculinity operates in much the same way as fallen femininity. Fallen masculinity as well as fallen femininity is within each one of us, whether we are a man or a woman. God spoke to Adam as He had spoken to Eve:

> *To Adam He said, "Because you listened to your wife and ate from the tree about which I commanded you, 'You must not eat of it,'*

> *Cursed is the ground because of you; through painful toil you will eat of it all the days of your life. It will produce thorns and thistles for you, and you will eat the plants of the field. By the sweat of your brow you will eat your food until you return to the ground, since from it you were taken; from dust you are and to dust you will return." (Gen 3:17-19).*

Thus, work became cursed. In the fallen male there is a drive to achieve and to get his identity from the ground – from work. The 'fallen masculine' very much enters into the toil and sweat of work because it is a mark of his identity. This is to be found in women too but it is nonetheless a trait of fallen masculinity. Both male and female can become workaholics, expressing the fallen masculinity that is trying to achieve its goals through the work of its hands and the sweat of its brow.

As a result, masculinity is expressed through domination and harshness. Without a vital connection to the heart everything becomes hard-line, driven, hard-bitten, hard-headed and utterly self-centred. Fallen masculinity can get incredibly locked into itself to the exclusion of others. Often women are just there to serve the needs and ambitions of men. Relationship becomes subservient to getting a man's needs met or to the goals that he is striving to achieve. Fallen masculinity is both heartless and restless – never content to 'be' but always 'doing' as a means of achieving an identity. It is aggressive and emotionally repressed. A major cause of depression is being cut off from our heart. Issues such as frigidity and pornography are symptomatic of disconnectedness from the heart.

We can observe a lot of 'fallen masculinity' within the culture of churches today. For example, an obvious form of this is where men fill all the leadership and ministry roles within the church, and women are not allowed to function in their gifting and callings. Some denominations even go as far as to assert that men have authority over *all* women, not just their wives! Many gifted women undoubtedly called by God have been wounded by the misinterpretation of certain Biblical passages, used to back up the prejudices of fallen masculinity. More subtle examples of fallen masculinity are within the style and culture of church life. A church that is overly locked into formulas, systems and programmes, or that is overly 'purpose-driven' is very much operating out of a fallen masculine bias.

Evidence of the Image in Nations and Cultures

What I love about understanding that the image of God encompasses masculinity and femininity is that we can see evidence of it everywhere. Much of what I observe now, I can see through this paradigm of 'the image' – the lens of the masculine and the feminine. Some years ago I began to realise that He had put His image into the different cultures in our world. It began to become clear to me that the masculine and feminine image was not just within individual human beings but it was resident within cultures. There are 'masculine' cultures and there are 'feminine' cultures.

Some examples that I would suggest of masculine cultures would be the English, German and Dutch cultures. These cultures historically have been very intellectual, very scientific, and very structured. They have been nations who, throughout history, have gone forth and conquered. Conversely, cultures such as the Celtic culture, the Scandinavian culture, and most indigenous cultures could be seen as being feminine cultures. These cultures are 'circular', earthy, and familial or tribal. A very striking example of the contrast between masculine and feminine mindsets would be the Greek culture as compared with the Hebrew culture.

My own nation, New Zealand, is a great example of both masculine and feminine cultures. Once, when I was praying for New Zealand, an unusually strong spirit of intercession came upon me for a uniting of culture between the indigenous Maori people and the majority who are of European descent. As clearly as anything I heard the Lord say to me, "Your land will be married," (Isa 62:4) bringing the masculine and the feminine into harmony. Within the context of New Zealand it suddenly became clear to me that the Maori people were like the mother in the land. When the Europeans came the Maori – a beautiful example of feminine culture – were already here. They are family-centred, connected to the land, very welcoming and hospitable. They are also a warlike people but in their case that is a feminine trait as it is primarily for defensive purposes. It is a mistake to think of feminine culture (or femininity for that matter) as being weak. If you want to find out what feminine strength is like, stand between a lioness and her cubs! Try and remove a bear cub from its mother! The ferocity of the feminine arising out of a protective and motherly instinct cannot be rivalled. So many feminine cultures are warlike cultures but they are not empire-building cultures. The feminine is warlike out of an instinct to protect its own. On the other hand, the masculine is warlike in order to expand its realm of rule.

This feminine ferocity is seen in experiences of other cultures that have been colonised. The indigenous people have risen up to defend themselves against their conquerors. However, because of fallenness, time and time again, the feminine (individually as well as culturally) has entered into the 'fallen masculine' to attempt to dominate the oppressor: "You have dominated us so we will turn round and dominate you!" Thus we see how this contributes to political activism or even guerrilla-type insurgencies and terrorism. These reactions do not express the true heart of the people, but are rather fallen expressions born out of violation and rejection. When femininity is wounded it can rise up in the 'fallen masculine'. God's intention was that both masculine cultures and feminine cultures would come together in harmony. He intended that the nations, in the ebb and flow of their femininity and masculinity, together would display His glory and dominion on the earth.

Many people are diverted from the point of this truth by focusing on their own balance of masculinity or femininity. Nothing can be changed by our own efforts, however. The whole point of this is to come out of a place of fallen masculinity and fallen femininity into Christ-likeness. As we become more and more like Jesus the true balance of masculinity and femininity is restored within the uniqueness of each individual as God has designed it to be.

3 | The War against the Feminine Image of God

Then the dragon was enraged at the woman...
Rev 12:17

Who is she that looks forth as the morning, fair as the moon, bright as the sun, terrible as an army with banners? Song of Sol 6:10

There has been an ancient war waged against femininity to this very day. Down through generations, civilisations and cultures, there has been a 'long war' against the feminine image of God to hinder the Church from ever realising the power and strength that we have been imbued with by God our Father. This subject is very dear to my heart. It contains a particularly personal and intimate part of my own story, which took me a long time to share with anybody. What I wish to write about is what I would call a 'maxi-truth' in that it contains understanding that spans from the beginning to the end. So let us first look at the beginning.

In Genesis 3: 1-3 we read:

Now the serpent was more crafty than any of the wild animals that God had made. He said to the woman, "Did God really say, 'You must not eat from any tree in the garden?' The woman said to the serpent, "We may eat fruit from the trees in the garden, but God did say, 'You must not eat fruit from the tree that is in the middle of the garden, and you must not touch it, or you will die.'

Picture the scene. The serpent and the woman are having this conversation.

At this point it is important to emphasise that the serpent was not merely a snake. In many religious pictures the scene in the Garden has been depicted with Adam and Eve standing under a tree around which a large snake is coiled, which whispers into Eve's ear. That is not the reality of what happened. Satan, or Lucifer was 'the Shining One'. The Hebrew word rendered 'serpent' is *nachash* from a root word, which means, "to shine." It wasn't until God cursed the serpent that it was confined to crawling on its belly and eating dust. There is much that can be said about this but that is not the main emphasis of this book.

It would be fair to say that, over the course of history, Eve has had a bad press, but my reading of this is different. I believe that Satan set out deliberately to deceive the woman. He did not appear to her as some vile creature. No, he *beguiled* her. There must have been something apparently innocent and initially attractive about the serpent that was able to gain Eve's trust. I believe that he wooed her over a period of time, gradually building a connection with her. The desire of a woman is to know and to be known in relationship. The Shining One knew that. He knew God and he had witnessed the act of creation. He knew only too well that he couldn't blithely approach someone who wanted deep mutual connection, in order to challenge her understanding of what God had said. I imagine that he came into the garden and said to her, "Aren't the trees looking beautiful this morning? I love how you have those flowers in the shade of the trees over there." He knew full well that she wouldn't just accept the word of a stranger and so he developed an ongoing dialogue with her – but it was a dialogue with an agenda.

The other thing to understand is this: This creature, Satan, had been there before the earth was created and he had a wealth of knowledge. Though cast out of the presence of God he still knew God extremely well and he had a master plan to defile and ultimately destroy the image of God. He couldn't destroy God but he could destroy God's image. He had put much thought and meticulous planning into this. I believe that he planned to create a relationship with the women and ultimately gain her trust. I suspect that a lot preceded what is actually recorded in the Scriptures. The narrative of the text has a context in which it is to be understood. However, Scripture generally only tells us what we need to know and it doesn't always go into great detail in terms of background and context.

So the woman replied to the serpent's probing question (probing her as to what God really did say) and, as we know, she misquoted what God had actually said. She has been much maligned for this misquote but, the truth is, she wasn't actually there when God had said it. He had given the prohibition to *the man*. Adam would have conveyed the message to his wife that they must not eat of the tree. Her knowledge was not first-hand: it was second-hand. My conviction is that she wasn't deliberately setting out to be cunning or disobedient. Notwithstanding all this, the fact remains that she did misquote what God had said.

The evil one then responded, "You shall not surely die!" (Gen 3:4) Scholars have informed me in conversation that the word 'you' is written in the plural form. This gives away the fact that the man, her husband, was standing beside her during her dialogue with the serpent. This is significant because we know that God had commanded him to protect the garden. That was innate to his masculinity, but he did not utter a word. Adam was passive when the serpent began to beguile Eve and twist the words of God. He did not make any move to correct Eve's misquotation.

Satan then promised the woman that when she ate of the fruit of the tree that she would receive understanding – that she would know as God knows!

When she saw that the tree was "good for food and pleasing to the eye and desirable for gaining wisdom – she took the fruit and ate it. Then she gave some to her husband who was with her and he ate it also." (Gen 3:6). Within femininity resides the desire to nurture and central to that is the desire to provide food. One of the ways in which women nurture their families is by providing and creating food for them to eat. The fact that it was pleasing to the eye also appealed to the innate appreciation of beauty that is contained within the feminine.

Eve saw that it was "desirable for gaining wisdom." Wisdom is always associated within Scripture as being a deeply feminine attribute. As we have noted, wisdom is actually personified as a woman in the Book of Proverbs.

We can appreciate then that she was looking at something that appealed greatly to her femininity. That was the very point at which the enemy attacked her. He knowingly and deliberately attacked her femininity.

With this context in place, let me look further on in the Genesis account. Verse 14 says:

So the Lord God said to the serpent, "Because you have done this,

"Cursed are you above all livestock and all wild animals! You will crawl on your belly and you will eat dust all the days of your life.

And I will put enmity between you and the woman, and between your offspring and hers; he will crush your head, and you will strike his heel.

At the point of mankind's ultimate failure God told the serpent that he would not be the ultimate victor – God would send a deliverer, the offspring of the woman, who would crush the serpent's head. The serpent would strike at his heel but he would crush the serpent's head. But, as I was reading this story one day, something occurred to me that I had never seen before. When I saw it, I felt as if a dagger was going through my heart. When I read what God had said, that He would put enmity between the serpent and the woman, I was devastated. It really crushed my heart.

I felt like a dagger had pierced my heart for this reason. This happened at a time when James and I were attempting to learn to know God the Father, and coming to believe that the true nature of God was that of a loving, heavenly father. You see, we all look at God the Father through the lens of our own individual experience, and my experience was that I had had a loving father. I was the apple of my father's eye but when I was 14 years old, one day my father came to me and said that he was leaving. He had met another woman and he was moving in with her and her three daughters. He reassured me that his love for me had not diminished but nevertheless he was still going to leave and move in with the other woman. He asked my permission, whether it was O.K. with me if he moved in with the other woman.

Of course, being his daughter, I wanted my father to be happy. I wanted to be the adult in this situation, never really believing in my own little heart that my father would actually leave me – and he kept saying, "It's not that I don't love you."

So this was my underlying picture of God the Father. I was content to stay with Jesus, happy to know and love Him, for the very reason that I did not – and could not – trust the Father. It was all very well to know that the Father loved me but it didn't really mean anything at all – because the day would inevitably come when He would say to me, "Denise, it's not that I don't love you. I *do* love you. I love you with great compassion *but* you are just not good enough to enter in. I'm sorry. I love you but our ways must part. You and I cannot be together."

I wasn't consciously aware that was how I was really feeling, but that was how my *heart* felt. It was a block that hindered me from coming to know the Father as He is meant to be known, because I could not trust His love for me. I knew that the day would surely come when there would be a parting of the ways.

When I read these verses in Genesis, that *God* would put enmity between the serpent and the woman – my heart was crushed. I saw that at the very outset of human existence upon this earth, God had placed enmity between Satan and women. From the very beginning the serpent is pitched against all that is feminine. I was devastated. I began to think of different cultures and civilisations throughout human history in which it was a distinct disadvantage to be a woman. Very quickly it was apparent to me that throughout the ages and in almost every corner of the globe, there was ample evidence of this enmity against womanhood. It could be seen as a sword of attack against women or even as a wall of resistance, but the enmity was undoubtedly there.

In talking about the war against the feminine, I can tell you that it is even waged against the feminine principle in males. As I outlined in the opening chapter, God has put femininity within men as well as women. There is a very specific attack against this aspect of a man's nature. When I speak about the war against femininity I am very careful to state that the attack does not originate in the human race. The war against the feminine is waged against men too. It is a war against the heart. It is pitted against anything that evokes love within us, against what makes us tender, compassionate, creative and nurturing. These characteristics have been largely belittled in much of Western culture. In contemporary Western culture many women tend to repress their femininity and seek to live from their masculine side, desiring to climb the corporate ladder, achieve success in a career, and defer or even abandon the idea of becoming a mother. There is no doubt that our culture is a predominantly masculine culture. Even though the status of women has improved dramatically over the last century, it still falls far short of equality.

Let me give some statistics here, which are eye-opening but nevertheless true. They are pretty much up-to-date and are taken from the most recent data collection and research. They only serve to underpin the truth of what I am saying. So here goes:

¤   According to estimates by the United Nations, up to 200 million woman and girls are demographically 'missing'. This term 'missing' disguises what is actually one of the most shocking crimes against humanity. The biological norm should be 100 newborn girls for every 103 newborn boys, and on that basis, millions more women should be living among us. If they are not they are 'missing' through being killed or through neglect and mistreatment and these deaths have gone unreported.[1]

---

1   This is taken from a report called *Women in an Insecure World: Violence Against Women – Facts, Figures and Analysis, 2005* edited by Marie Vlachova and Lea Biason for the Geneva Centre Democratic Control of Armed forces. It comments further that this statistic "implies that each year 1.5 to 3 million

¤ Thirty-nine thousand girls die annually in China because parents don't give them the same medical care and attention that they give to boys – and that is infants at one year old and under.[2]

¤ The number of women forced or sold into prostitution is estimated at anywhere between 700,000 and 4 million per year. Between 120,000 and 500,000 of them are sold to pimps and brothels in Europe alone. Profits from the sex slavery market are estimated at US$7 – 12 billion per year.[3]

¤ In 2010, 8391 dowry death cases were reported across India, meaning a bride was burned every 90 minutes, according to statistics recently released by the National Crime Records Bureau. A decade earlier this number was 6995, but climbed to 8093 dowry deaths in 2007.[4]

¤ Between 100 and 140 million girls and women are living with the effects of female genital mutilation.[5] The practice, widespread in Africa, is intended, among other things, to reduce unfaithfulness in women, though other myths have evolved to justify the practice which deforms millions of girls each year, kills some and creates serious infections in others. The custom thrives despite it being illegal.

---

girls and women are killed through gender related violence. In comparison 2.8 million die of AIDS, 1.27 of malaria. Or, put in the most horrible terms: violence against women causes every 2 to 4 years a mountain of corpses equal to the Jewish Holocaust."

2   Kristof, Nicholas D & Wudunn, S, *Half The Sky: How to Change the World,* (Virago Press, 2010).

3   From the same report as previous note. It further comments that in some countries such as Moldova sex trafficking is of such proportions that it is threatening to destabilise the population equilibrium.

4   Reported in *The Daily Telegraph* 27 February 2012. "Indian Dowry Deaths on the Rise."

5   UNICEF, *Female Genital Mutilation Cutting Factsheet.*

◻ Nearly 90,000 people reported being raped in the United States in 2008. The U.S Bureau of Justice Statistics states that 91% of victims are female and 9% are male.

◻ The World Health Organisation estimates that globally one woman in five will be the victim of rape or attempted rape in her lifetime.[6] Other data suggests that in Canada, New Zealand, the United Kingdom and the United States the corresponding figure is one in six women.[7] In South Africa a frightening 40 per cent of girls aged 17 or under are reported to have been the victim of rape or attempted rape.[8] This translates globally into a staggering (yet conservative) estimate that the number of victims is estimated at 700 million girls and women.

◻ The impact of conflict on women is different than it is on men. Sexual violence as a tactic of warfare has been used systematically and deliberately for centuries. It is used against civilian populations to destroy the social fabric of communities, as a deliberate measure to infect the victims with HIV, for the purpose of enforced impregnation, and to displace and terrorise communities. In Rwanda, it is estimated that between 250,000 and 500,000 women were raped in less than a 100 days as part of the 1994 genocide, in which 800,000 were killed.[9]

These statistics make for shocking reading but they demonstrate vividly that there has been a war waged against women and it is still raging fiercely today. Globally, it is women who suffer the greatest injustice in the workplace.

---

6   WHO, *Violence Against Women Factsheet* No.239, 2000.

7   UNDP, Human Development Report, 1995: *Gender and Human Development,* p7.

8   UN Habitat, *State of the World's Cities: Trends in Sub-Saharan Africa,* p4.

9   From the report, *In Pursuit of Justice, Progress of the World's Women,* 2011-2012 by the United Nations Entity for Gender Equality and the Empowerment of Women.

According to the same UN report about the impact of conflict on women, more than half the world's working women are in vulnerable employment, trapped in insecure jobs and outside the cover of labour legislation. In the developing world, more than one third of women are married and childbearing before the age of eighteen, thus missing out on education. In developing countries, the leading causes of death for girls aged fifteen to nineteen are directly linked to pregnancy and childbirth. On a global scale, the vast majority of women fall outside of legislation affecting women's rights in the workplace.

Often, our Western culture has created a scenario in which both father and mother are absent from the home because they are both pursuing careers. My daughter, Amanda, who lives in Sydney, is a full-time mother and she shared with me about the questions that she constantly faced from other women. They would question her as to what her occupation was, to which she replied,

"I'm a full-time mother."

"Yes, but what do you *actually* do?"

"I stay at home to look after the children."

"But you must have a job!"

It was as if being a full-time mother was insufficient to validate Amanda as a person. In other words, unless you have a successful career you are not living a full life. Many of these values such as nurture (long held in times gone by) are no longer cherished. There is a war against femininity whereby we are ashamed to own up to having compassion or tenderness towards someone, e.g., within the office environment. The 'office nerd' is often a figure of ridicule. We push the weaker to the edge of, or even beyond, the group. Anyone who stands up for the rights of the underdog will find themselves to be unpopular. The tender and genuinely heartfelt values are rubbished and maligned. This is having an immense effect on Western culture in particular. Even when I was a child growing up, the education of women and girls was not valued or given priority. Women were not seen as having equal intelligence to men.

In many countries, particularly in the developing world, girls are deprived of education. In almost every region of the world women are more likely to be 'education poor' – to have four years or less of primary education – than young men. A report by the Global Campaign for Education in February 2012 states that "in 47 out of 54 African countries, girls have less than 50% chance of completing primary school...only four in ten Pakistani women over the age of 15 can read and write, compared to 70% men," and two thirds of the world's 76 million non-literate adults are women.

As I was thinking about what the Scripture says, that God will put enmity between the serpent and the woman, I could clearly see the reality of this outworked throughout the ages and in every corner of the globe. There has been a war against femininity and it has been against men also but the truth is that it has been particularly intense against women, because women contain more of the feminine image of God. When this shocking catalogue of statistics and data came to my notice, I spent many days and nights crying out to God, saying, "How can I believe that You love me equally, as a daughter, when You have set the enemy against me? You have set the enemy against femininity. How can I have confidence in Your love for me?"

It was a *huge* problem for me, an obstacle that I could not surmount. Even when I considered Western civilisation (which is predominantly American culture) there is systemic repression of women. In my own nation, New Zealand, equal rights, to this day, are still not fully established for women. Women still cannot receive the same pay as men for working in an equivalent position in the workplace. When my mother was working, at one point she had five men working under her supervision, who were all on a higher salary than she was!

So I faced a big dilemma. I was wrestling with the dichotomy of how God could love me equally on the one hand yet be seen to clearly favour masculinity and the masculine way on the other. I knew that it was not always this way. In the garden, before the Fall, there was complete harmony between the man and his wife, a synthesis of male and female, masculine and feminine. After the Fall we see that disharmony and division came between the man and his wife; in the words of C. S. Lewis, "a sword fell between the sexes."[10] It was *after* the Fall that God said, "Your desire shall be for your husband and he will rule over you." But when Jesus, the second Adam, came He reinstated what God had appointed at the beginning. I believe that God would have conveyed something like this when He gave Eve to Adam: "You will not rule over her but You will love her, and lay down your life for her. You will cherish her and co-rule with her." The second Adam re-established what the first Adam had lost – the laying down of a man's life for his wife.

As I was in this dilemma another thought began to occur to me. What about the Church? How did the Church treat women? What was the prevailing attitude to women throughout the ages of the history of the church? I was soon to discover what the prevailing view throughout church history was. Let me quote some statements from some of the most notable figures in the history of the Church.[11]

---

10   C.S. Lewis, *A Grief Observed*, (Faber and Faber, 1961).

11   Sourced by Stephen Hill and Dr. Neil Whitehead.

- Clement of Alexandria (c. 150-220 AD) believed that every woman should blush because she is a woman and that a man's beard was a sign of his superiority over woman. He stated, "Nothing for men is shameful, for man is endowed with reason; but for women it brings shame even to reflect on what her nature is."

- Tertullian (160 to 240 AD), the father of Latin theology, stated that, "You are the gateway of the devil: you are the one who unseals the curse of that tree, and you are the first one to turn your back on the divine law...you are the one who persuaded him whom the devil was not capable of corrupting; you easily destroyed the image of God, Adam. Because of what you deserve, that is death, even the Son of God had to die. And do you still think of adorning yourself above and beyond your tunics of animal skin? The judgment of God upon this sex (woman) lives on in this age, therefore, necessarily the guilt should live on also."

- Origen (185 to 254 AD), the church's first systematic theologian actually castrated himself.   This has been attributed to him: "...a woman is not permitted to speak in an assembly...men should not sit and listen to a woman...even if she says admirable things, or even saintly things, that is of little consequence, since they come from the mouth of a woman." He is also quoted as saying, "...God does not stoop to look upon what is feminine and of the flesh."

- Ambrose of Milan (340 to 397 AD) recognised in 1298 as one of the four original 'Doctors of the Church' and one of the most influential ecclesiastic figures of the fourth century said, "She who does not have faith is a woman and should be called by the name of her sex but if she progresses to perfect manhood she then does away with the name of her sex."

▢ Augustine (AD 354–430) who has the reputation of being the 'greatest of the Fathers of the Western Church', whose thought has laid the foundation of Western theology, believed that man and woman when married were the image of God. However, he also believed that a man on his own was still the full image of God, whereas the woman outside of marriage was not in God's image.[12] He placed the blame for the fall squarely upon women's shoulders. He even accused woman as being the cause of the Flood![13]

▢ Thomas Aquinas (1225-1274), known as the 'Angelic Doctor', taught that the woman did not possess the image of God in the same way as a man and is therefore spiritually inferior. He held the view that, "Woman is defective and misbegotten... Naturally subject to man... and in subjection to the law of nature but a slave is not." thus asserting that a slave can be freed but a woman never!

▢ Martin Luther (1483-1546), the well-known Protestant reformer, said, "Woman must neither begin or complete anything without man. Where he is, there she must be, and bend before him as before a master, whom she shall fear and to whom she shall be subject and obedient." He also said, "Men have broad shoulders and narrow hips, and accordingly they possess intelligence. Women have narrow shoulders and broad hips. Woman ought to stay

---

12 "...so that that whole substance may be one image; but when she is referred separately to her quality of help-meet, which regards the woman herself alone, then she is not the image of God; but as regards the man alone, he is the image of God as fully and completely as when the woman too is joined with him in one." From Chapter 7 of Book 12 *On the Holy Trinity.*

13 This can be referenced from Augustine's *The City of God,* Book 15, Part 22, "...and this calamity, as well as the first, was occasioned by woman."

at home; the way they were created indicates this, for they have broad hips and a wide fundament to sit upon, keep house and bear and raise children."

These examples span more than a thousand years of Church history from early times through to the Reformation. Needless to say, misogyny in the Church continued unabated beyond the Reformation into the Modern era and right down to this day.

And so it goes on! Misogyny had inevitably found its way into the Church. The Church became part of Satan's armoury in the war against the feminine image of Father God. All of us have experienced and can readily point to examples of misogyny in our own Christian experience. Even in the local church that we were members of for quite some time, it was held that a woman could only be used in the gift of prophecy if the prophetic word had been initially given to her husband but he failed to express it. Then the 'gift' would transfer to his wife so that she could speak it out in the congregation! It was inconceivable that God would speak directly to and through a woman! Following that logic a woman found herself in a Catch 22 situation because, by giving the prophecy, she was uncovering the disobedience of her husband.

Many churches *still* do not permit women to hold any office of leadership. So, although the Church is recognised spiritually as 'the Bride of Christ', any expression of femininity is repressed. The way that a church functions is very often much more masculine than feminine. The Church is often depicted as an army going forth to war – going forth to conquer. Many churches have no other *raison d'etre* or mode of functioning than to conquer. There is certainly a commission to save the lost, but the point that I am making here is this: God is also *feminine by nature* and His intention is that the Church should display that femininity.

I do not think it is too strong to say that the whole world is the way it is because of misogyny. Hatred of femininity has come through every major civilisation. Since the Fall it has undoubtedly been a masculine world. The Church has actually made a point of emphasising misogyny. Many of the great fathers and theologians of the Church have combined revelation and great intellect to establish doctrinal foundation upon which our theology rests today. However, their attitudes towards women display a shocking bigotry in statements that seem inconsistent with their other teachings. The subject of women seems to stir up a vitriolic hatred coming from deep, emotional anger rather than well thought-out intellectual arguments, e.g., many theologians, when considering the terminology of God as 'mother' are especially vehement in their rejection of such a term. Why does this cause such fury? Why does it stir up such negative emotions? I believe it is because of misogyny. It goes beyond mere intellectual debate and is taken as an insult to God that any feminine traits should be attributed to Him. Why? Because femininity is despised and seen as inherently inferior to masculinity, and it is therefore unthinkable for the misogynistic mindset to attribute femininity to the Godhead. The underlying presumption is that femininity is somehow less valuable than masculinity. If Jesus is the 'second Adam' then the Church's calling is to be 'the second Eve'. Spiritually speaking, the Church is called to be 'the mother of all living' on the earth – that is her destiny. God wants to establish the Church to be the mother of all living, the life-giver, the one who feeds, nurtures, and creates. She is to be the one who gives form to others so that they become all that God has created them to be.

The Church has often been described as a hospital – a place where the bruised and broken can come and receive healing. Yet, there is more to it. Paul says the Church is called to display "the manifold" (all-varied or multi-faceted) wisdom of God to the "rulers and authorities in the heavenly realms."(Eph 3:10). So often, tragically, we only see a masculine expression of who God is. That is only one facet. The femininity of God is lacking in expression in the life of the Church. We see people going out to 'win the lost' but having no compassion for them. We see churches attempting to 'build the Kingdom' but the motivation of heart-compassion is not there. When Jesus looked upon the lost, He was deeply moved with compassion, seeing them as "sheep without a shepherd"(Mat 9:36). The life and ministry of Jesus was an overflow of the compassion and tenderness that was in His heart. Jesus expressed in its fullness both the masculine and the feminine image of the Father.

Let me tell you something of my own story. When I first became a Christian I began to read a lot of books. One book in particular that impacted me greatly was a book by Jean Vanier, called *Community and Growth*.[14] In that book, Jean Vanier used a term that really captured my imagination. He used the term, "our deepest wound."[15] As I read this I asked the Lord, "Lord, what is my deepest wound?" I figured that the Lord would immediately show me the answer to my question and that I would continue life as normal after that. I would live my life as before, while knowing what my deepest wound was. But the Lord didn't answer my question; He never revealed to me what my deepest wound was.

---

14   Jean Vanier founded the L'Arche community in 1964. It has grown to be an international network of communities for people with intellectual disabilities.

15   "In community life we discover our own deepest wound and learn to accept it....It is from this very wound that we are born." p18

I went through many years of frustration – and all the time God was working in my life – but I never got the answer to my question, What is my deepest wound?

However, when He began to take me on this journey that I am writing about now – showing me the ancient enmity of the serpent against the feminine image of God, I began to think more and more about my own life experience.

When I was a child I spent a lot of time with my maternal grandmother. Quite often I stayed in her house for periods of time. She was everything I wanted to be. When I was staying with her, she would come into my bedroom every night and listen to me saying my prayers. I would say, "Gentle Jesus, meek and mild, look upon this little child . God bless Mummy, God bless Daddy, God bless my family. Make Denise a good girl. Amen!" I think it was her who taught me to say, "Make Denise a good girl!" She was very loving and nurturing, and I loved her very much. But while I was staying with her, a guest would from time to time stay over at her house. This man began to molest me sexually, beginning when I was quite young and continuing through-out the years.

One night, when my grandmother was listening to my bedtime prayers, I blurted out what this particular man had been doing to me – the most recent being on that very day! My poor grandmother got such a shock when she heard this that she jumped back, her eyes widened and she put her finger across her lips and began backing out through the door. She gasped, "Shhh, Shhh, Shhhh! Don't tell anyone! No one is going to believe you!" And as she got out through the doorway she hurriedly whispered, "It doesn't matter! It doesn't matter!" and disappeared from view. That was all I heard. Nothing more was said. I believed that it didn't matter.

I found out many years later that the reason why she said, "It doesn't matter!" – apart from not really knowing how else to respond – was because she really meant that she was going to fix this situation, and put a stop to the molestation. As I said, it took me 40 years or so to find out what she *really* meant when she uttered the words, "It doesn't matter!"

However, the abuse didn't stop. It carried on as before. Many years later I asked my mother why no-one had stepped in to stop the abuse. On hearing this, my mother was deeply distressed because she thought that it had stopped! Apparently there had been a family meeting after I had told my grandmother what was happening to me. They confronted this person and told him to stop it. But they didn't come and tell me about this, the man ignored them, and the abuse went on. With the abuse continuing unabated, I was left with the words, "It doesn't matter!" ringing in my ears. These words became repetitious in my head. Many victims of abuse develop a little mantra, which they repeat to themselves to disassociate from what is happening to them. My little mantra became, "It doesn't matter. It doesn't matter. It doesn't matter." I remember looking up at the ceiling of my bedroom and saying it over and over to myself, "It doesn't matter. It doesn't matter. It doesn't matter!" And that was how I got through.

The interesting thing is this; over the years I have counselled hundreds of men and women who have been sexually abused. I never forgot that I too was sexually abused – but somehow it didn't matter! It didn't matter to the point that sometimes I was actually quite puzzled at the distress of those who had suffered sexual abuse. I wondered why I wasn't affected in the same way as the person sitting in front of me. It just passed through my mind that I had also been abused, but that was all.

The years passed by. My father had walked out on our family and gone to live with another woman. Then something else happened.

One night, I was babysitting for a friend whose marriage had also broken up. Our friend had five children ranging from two years old to twelve years old. The year was around 1960 and there was no television in the house. She had gone to the movies with another friend and I was left in the house, responsible for the children. I was 14 years of age.

All of a sudden there was a knock at the door. When I opened it, a man was standing there. He was obviously drunk, swaying unsteadily on his feet, holding himself up against the wall. He introduced himself as a friend of the owner of the house. Even though the man was a complete stranger to me, I invited him inside and offered to make him a cup of tea.

As soon as he entered, without any hesitation he grabbed me, pushed me to the floor and proceeded to rape me. And, in the midst of this trauma, all I could think was – "It doesn't matter!"

What was more terrifying for me was the responsibility that I felt for the children in my charge. In those days I was fairly naive as regards matters of sexuality and I was terrified by what was happening to me. But I didn't recognise how significant it really was. My greatest concern, however, was what he might do next, to the children. What would he do to them *after he had finished with me*? How was I going to fight him off? How was I going to stop him doing this to the twelve year old? What would he do to the seven-year old? The five-year old? The two-year old? Fortunately, I didn't have to worry about that much longer for he very soon fell asleep and slept until our friend returned home.

I didn't tell anyone then about what had happened to me. In our town at the time there was a rape case going through the court. But the talk of the town was not about the rapist; it was about the girl who had been raped. Was she somehow responsible? What did she do to entice him? Did she lead him on or seduce him in some way? What was she wearing that he couldn't resist? Did she somehow communicate that it was O.K? Also at that time my mother and father were going through a divorce. I was broken-hearted about my father abandoning the family. The family was going through a distressing time and I felt that I couldn't add another problem to the mix. So I kept telling myself that it didn't matter, bottled it up and said nothing. I remember walking to school, kicking the stones as I walked and repeating my mantra the whole way to school, "It doesn't matter, it doesn't matter, it doesn't matter, it doesn't matter."

So life went on. Then, after James and I got married, years later we ended up pastoring a church. I had initially refused to join James in leading the church (because we had been through burnout) but I couldn't resist a growing love for the people so I ended up going along with James and pastoring the church together with him. Then one day, one of the church members approached me and said, "Denise, I would like you to come to a conference that I am organising." The conference would be hosting a group called Desert Streams Ministries, which ran a programme known as *Living Waters*. They were American and, at that time, were not in Australia or New Zealand. This man, however, had been through the programme in the U.S. and believed that the body of Christ in New Zealand really needed this. The Living Waters programme ministered to the sexually and relationally broken. I figured that included all of us, for none of us are perfect sexually or relationally, so my initial instinct was to turn down the invitation. I didn't want to go to *yet another* Christian conference. However, I subsequently changed my mind and went reluctantly because I felt that it was my duty to go for the sake of the congregation. I had agreed to co-pastor alongside James, after all. So I said to the Lord, "Lord, if there is anything in me that You want to touch or heal, I will own it, no matter what it is," and I went along to the conference.

At the conference, inevitably the session came one evening, where the subject focused on sexual abuse. The speaker spoke about how sexual abuse affects us: our selves, our relationships, our marriages, indeed our whole lives. He spoke about what the cost is to us. You see, before we can really forgive our abuser and be free, we need to realise how much it has cost us. Sexual abuse has been very costly for a lot of people. The reality of the cost for some is that they cannot sustain an intimate relationship. For others it means that they are never able to be fully communicative in the sexual relationship.

And then the speaker said, "Now for those of you who have been sexually abused, I want you to stand." My first thought, as always, was, "Well, I don't need to stand because it didn't affect me." Then the Holy Spirit came and said, "Hold on! Remember our talk in the car. I thought you said that you would own whatever I wanted to put My finger on, even if it was something little." So, when the people stood up, I stood up too. The speaker began by saying, "I want to stand in a place of intercession and stand in the place of your abuser – as a man – and ask you to forgive me for the abuse that happened to you...because it really mattered!"

When he said those words, "...*because it really mattered*" I was completely floored. It was like a punch in the stomach. Nothing else could have cut through but those words, "It really mattered!"

My chin almost hit my knees! My legs buckled, and I fell over so fast that before I knew it I was in a crouching posture. All of the pent up emotion of all the years began to rise up from the depths of my soul in a great river of tears. It felt as if the tears were coming from my feet, up through my body, and were being forcibly ejected through my eyes. I was crying so hard that I felt like my face was coming off. I cried for what seemed like an eternity. The memory of the rape, the trauma of which was suppressed under my denial for many years, came sharply into my consciousness. All of the feelings of powerlessness and helplessness, the vulnerability and the pain, rushed out. I felt like rivers were streaming out of my eyes. My tear ducts were too small to contain the torrent of tears that was coursing out from my eyes. I wept and wept and wept.

While I was lying on the floor, as the crying was subsiding and peace was beginning to settle within me, I heard the Lord speak to me. I heard it so clearly in my spirit. He said, *"Denise – this is your deepest wound! Your deepest wound is being a woman."*

When He said that to me I knew that I knew that I knew that He was right!

Right from when I was little, from very early in my life, I knew that it wasn't good to be a girl. Even before the abuse started I wanted to be a boy. I had always been known as a tomboy, competing with the boys in my class and in the street where I lived. I was always invited to be on the boys' team, picked ahead of other boys. I was picked because I was such an accomplished 'boy.' I could run well, throw well, catch well. I was agile and adept at the games boys play. My identity was very masculine. I wanted to be strong. I wanted to be able to stand on my own. I knew very early on that I wanted to be independent because I could not depend on anyone else to protect me. I wanted to make my own life happen. I wanted to create my own world. But this was all because I didn't want to be vulnerable. I didn't want the vulnerability of being 'a little girl'. Compounded with this, there was the sexual molestation and the rape, and the powerlessness of not being able to defend myself and having no-one to defend me.

So, with all the tears coming out, God so kindly said to me, "*This* is your deepest wound. Being a woman is your deepest wound." And I knew that He was absolutely right. When He said those words I can only describe what happened next like this: it was like being baptised in femininity. A rush of femininity enveloped me. He filled me with what had been missing in me. I was completely filled with the desire to be feminine, and not to be ashamed of it. All the shame of being 'the fallen woman' flowed away with the tears. It just left me.

When He spoke those words He baptised me in true femininity – a femininity that is not weak. The Song of Solomon says of the beloved bride:

> *You are beautiful, my darling, as Tirzah, lovely as Jerusalem, majestic as troops with banners...(6:4)... Who is this that appears like the dawn, fair as the moon, bright as the sun, majestic as the stars in procession?" (6:10).*

There is something in femininity that is beautiful and gentle, but it has a strength – a strength that is different from masculine strength, an inner strength that cannot be walked over, that is not able to be subdued and conquered, but rather yields of its own volition. There is a strength in femininity that comes from the inside. The strength in masculinity comes from the outside, from what is external, but the true femininity that is in God has strength that comes from the inside. God baptised me with that femininity, which comes from Him.

I returned home after this encounter and told my family everything. I told them all that had happened. I told them about the sexual abuse. I told them about being raped. And I recounted how God had amazingly healed me. A little while later I was doing something very ordinary – I certainly wasn't praying – and God spoke to me again. I heard His voice so clearly in my spirit. When God speaks you know exactly what He is speaking about. I heard Him say: "Go back and have another look and tell Me who I am speaking to."

Immediately I knew that He was talking about the third chapter of Genesis. He was talking about that verse which says, "I will put enmity between you and the woman."

As soon as He said that I knew what He meant. In my brokenness I had completely misinterpreted what this verse was actually talking about. If He had been addressing the woman it would have meant exactly what I had always in-terpreted it to mean. But He wasn't speaking to the woman! He was speaking to the serpent! Immediately I received a picture in my mind about what was happening right there in the garden. I had always imagined how disappointed God was. We hear a lot about the 'broken heart of God' and that was what coloured my view of what had happened. I am sure that the depths of God's feelings cannot be fathomed but He never lost His love and His compassion for his children.

I had always imagined Him standing *alongside* the serpent and saying to the woman, "Well, now you are going to have pain in childbirth and I am going to make you suffer. Your husband will dominate you." I imagined that all the things that the early Church fathers had said about women were really just a repetition of what God had originally said to the woman and, by extension, to all women. "Because you have done this the man will completely dominate you, and rightly so! And what is more, you deserve it!"

But that is *not* what happened. When He spoke, I saw Him taking a step – to stand *with* the woman and *with* her husband. And from *that* standing point, He addressed the serpent.

The conversation had been between the serpent and the woman but that was only one battle. It may have been 'round one' to the serpent but the war was by no means over. The serpent had indeed won the initial skirmish against the woman when she ate of the fruit of the tree, but we see the bigger picture when God the Father says to the serpent: "You think that you have won. You believe that you have corrupted and defiled My image *but* I am going to put enmity between you and the woman, and between your seed and hers."

Do you know who the woman actually is in this story? The woman is the Church – the Second Eve. We know that the seed of the woman speaks of Jesus, but the woman speaks of the Church and it is the Church who will ultimately defeat the enemy. That is the way God sees it. Down through the years the serpent has perpetuated the great lie that God set him against us. The whole world has been led astray by this deception. But one day we will look at him and say: "Is *this* the one that ruled the earth?" It is incredible that we have let him deceive us and exercise authority over us. Thank God, the Holy Spirit is bringing revelation as to the true nature of our place and our authority in Christ. The whole story is that he is not so much our enemy as we are *his* enemy. The boot is on the other foot, so to speak. He hasn't been set against us – as I thought Genesis 3.15 was saying – rather we have been set *against him*.

Don't let him lie to you that he has some legitimate and God-given authority in your life. Don't believe that Satan has some inalienable right to harass you and keep you from entering into your full inheritance as a son and daughter of God. No! His lie to us as been that he is our enemy but God clearly shows that the reverse is true. *We are his enemy.* Peter says that the enemy goes around "like a roaring lion, seeking whom he may devour" (1Pe 5:8). He is not a roaring lion; he is only *like* a roaring lion. Someone once said that we need to say to Satan, "You can't roar. You can only hiss!" Satan loves to masquerade that he actually has authority over the believer and, as long as he is successful in his deception, he can wield a certain amount of power. But as we come into the realisation of how God really sees it, we will find more and more that his lies have no power over us. The truth is, beloved, *we* are *his* nemesis! (Rom16:20).

Some years ago when James and I were ministering in Minneapolis, two intercessors came to me after the meeting and began to pray for me. They were deeply moved, so much so that they took hold of my ankles and began to cry out loudly. Then one of them proclaimed: *"When the true feminine is restored the Bride will be revealed!"*

Think about that! When the true and full image of God is restored, then the Bride of Christ will rise up in her authority over all the power of the enemy. She will crush Satan under her heel. This is the reason why the enemy has been so vociferous in his attack against femininity because he knows that if he can destroy the nurturer then he can destroy the heart of the next generation. Why? Because it is the nurturer who brings forth the heart. It is femininity that puts the heart into humanity. The body of Christ has historically been very strong in 'the head' but now our heart is being made alive. Many of us as individuals are completely out of touch with our hearts. We don't know where to find our hearts, or how to operate from the heart. The Lord is restoring this ability to us both individually and corporately.

The restoration of the true feminine, the coming forth of the feminine image of God, is a huge issue because the *Bride is feminine.* However, it must be said that femininity is strongest *in women* and we have not valued that. Men have not valued that, and women have not valued that. I myself hated femininity and the fact that I was a woman. The Church has not valued it, and neither has society. All of humanity has participated knowingly and unknowingly in misogyny, in the attack against the feminine. Men and women need to take steps to release, to value, and to honour the feminine. The feminine has been exploited and taken advantage of by the fallen masculine tendency to dominate and take over. Part of the mandate of our ministry is to bring a revelation of this, and to see repentance on behalf of the domination of masculinity so that the true image of God – both masculine and feminine – can be restored in its glory. It is vitally important that the true femininity within *both* men *and* women is restored so that we can become all that God intended the Bride of Christ to be.

4| The Two Paradigms

The dance which we dance is at the centre and for the dance all things were made. C.S. Lewis

God, in His love, desires intimate relationship with His creation, mankind. That has been His desire from a past eternity. It was why He created, and it was why He redeemed through the death of His Son on the cross. His great purpose is that we should come into a place of being united with Him. There is a central and vital relationship that we have been created for – a relationship which is our eternal destiny. The astounding truth is that we have been created to be part of the relationship that is at the centre of all things – the Trinity. We have been created out of the mutual love that is in the Godhead and that selfsame love relationship is our destiny. Let me, in this chapter, pursue this wonderful truth of our identity in God a little further.

We well know that there are many different terms that are used when describing God. For example, take a term such as "Ancient of Days." There are also many titles that are given to Jesus such as "King of kings" and "Lord of lords." These terms are rightly used for God is indeed the One who existed before all things. Jesus is and will always be Lord and King, but within the spectrum of intimate and family relationship, we know God by two different relational paradigms. One paradigm is that of God as 'father' – and the other paradigm is that of God as 'bridegroom'. These are the two ways in which we will live in intimacy with God eternally.

The foundation for both of these paradigms is set down in Genesis 2:7:

> *And the Lord God formed man from the dust of the ground and breathed into his nostrils the breath of life, and man became a living being.*

The creation of Adam is really the first picture of God becoming 'father' on the earth. In the genealogy of Jesus in Luke's Gospel, Adam is referred to as "the son of God" (Luk 3:38). Genesis 2 describes the beginnings and the formation of God's fatherhood as experienced by human beings on the earth.

Most of what we teach in our ministry has really come out of questions that James and I have asked God. Over the years we have questioned God about many things in life and in the Scriptures that we do not understand; and God, in His own time – sometimes it takes years – has come back with answers. Those answers are always rich with revelation and significance.

I can remember asking God a question, which came out of reading the second chapter of Genesis. In verse 18, God said, "It is not good for the man to be alone. I will make a helper suitable for him." I remember reading that and thinking, "God, You know the end from the beginning. You know all things. If You knew that a time was coming when You would see that it was not good for the man to be alone – why didn't You make the two (man and woman) to begin with? Why didn't You create them together – the man and his wife?"

We don't actually know how long Adam was alone but, however long it was, we do know that God said that it was not good for him to be alone. Then God made a helper for the man. The word 'helper' in the original language is used many times in connection with God Himself, for example, "God is my helper." (Psa 54:4) or, "... a very present *help* in trouble" (Psa 46:1). It is the same root word (*ezer* in Hebrew), which is used here in Genesis when God said, "I will make a helper suitable for him." So it follows that the 'suitable helper' for Adam, the woman, will be a helper that would reflect the way that God helps.

So I was asking God this question – why didn't He make the man and his wife together at the beginning? Why did He wait to create the woman? It took many years before God answered me. I think there is a reason why He does this. I believe it is because we often have a lot to learn in order to understand the real answer to the question. Sometimes we ask questions of God – but if He told us the answer straight away we wouldn't understand it. We wouldn't get the fullness of understanding that God wants us to have. So He waits until we have a greater foundation of understanding within us so that we can receive more revelation.

When God eventually answered my question, it was revealed to me that Genesis 2:18 was describing a reality much greater and much deeper than just Adam and his wife. It was describing God as Father, Jesus as Bridegroom, and the Church as the bride. I can remember meditating upon these two paradigms – God as father and God as bridegroom – and I wondered, "God, how does this actually function? How does it work in eternity?" – because knowing God as father is a huge reality in itself. In fact, you could almost say that it is all-fulfilling!

Alongside this, I was deeply aware of a profound experience in my own life some years earlier when I had what can only be described as a staggering revelation of Jesus as the divine Bridegroom. It was a mystical and deeply 'romantic' experience in a spiritual sense. I knew beyond any shadow of doubt that Jesus *is* the Bridegroom for all time and for eternity. Earthly fathers are meant to be a depiction of what God the Father is like. Similarly, husbands are to depict what the heavenly Bridegroom and Husband is really like. Fallenness has marred all of this but that does not detract from God's intention that fathers and husbands are to reflect the eternal fatherhood and the eternal husbanding that is supremely in God Himself.

I remember the night that He answered my question. We were staying in Wisconsin and we were in a little house meeting. It was the middle of winter and everything was covered in a blanket of snow. We could see snow sitting on the trees, lit up by the reflected light coming from the house in the stillness of the night. We were in the midst of a time of worship and I was gazing out of the window on the beautiful and serene setting that reminded me of C.S. Lewis's Narnia. As I was worshipping Him the Lord suddenly spoke to me. It was many years since I had asked Him that question but I knew immediately that what He said was in direct response to my question all that time earlier.

He said to me:

Denise, the reason that you don't understand is because you think that it's all about you. It's about a Father in eternity who wanted to give a bride to His Son – and so He created you. And it is about a Son in eternity who wanted to give many sons to His Father – and so He created you! You are the gift of the Son to the Father – and the gift of the Father to the Son.

Darrell W. Johnson, in his book *Experiencing the Trinity*, makes this statement, which has impacted me greatly:

> *At the centre of the universe is a relationship...It is out of that relationship that you and I were created and redeemed. And it is for that relationship that you and I were created and redeemed![1]*

That is our destiny! There is a lot of talk these days about finding our destiny but *that* is our destiny! Our destiny is to be a part of the Trinity! Not to be of the same substance of course, but to be caught up into that relationship! As we are in the Son, we are in that place! We are in Christ, before the Father's face. This is what we have been created for. That is why we sometimes say – don't worry about getting a vision to be a prophet or an apostle! As wonderful as that may be, it will all pass away, but your destiny and my destiny is much greater and will *never* pass away. Our destiny, through grace, is to have a part with the Trinity itself! That is what we have been created for. That is what Jesus paid a price for, so that we might be a part of the fellowship between the Father and the Son eternally.

Father Raniero Cantlamessa, Preacher to the Papal Household, writes in his book, *Life in Christ:*

> *We are involved in the incessant motion of reciprocal giving and receiving between the Father and the Son from whose jubilant embrace the Holy Spirit springs, who then brings down to us a spark of this fire of love.*

He goes on to recount the story of, "...someone, who, through grace, experienced this." When James had the privilege of meeting Father Cantalamessa, he put to him directly whether or not he (Fr. Cantalamessa) was the

---

1   Darrell W Johnson, *Experiencing the Trinity,* (Regent College Publishing, 2002).

'someone' who had this experience. Father Cantalamessa evaded the question and would not give an unequivocal answer one way or the other. In the book he recounts the experience as follows:

One night I felt the great tenderness of the Father enveloping me in a sweet and gentle embrace. Beside myself, I knelt down huddled in the dark. My heart was pounding and I abandoned myself completely to his will. And the Holy Spirit introduced me to the love of the Trinity. Also through me the ecstatic exchange of giving and receiving was taking place between Christ, with whom I was united, and the Father, and between the Father and the Son. But how can the inexpressible be expressed? I saw nothing, but it was much more than seeing and there are no words to explain this jubilant exchange which was responding, soaring, receiving and giving. And from that exchange an intense life flowed from one to the other like the warm milk coming from a mother's breast to her child. And I was that child and so was all creation that partakes of life, of the kingdom, of glory as it had been regenerated by Christ. Opening the Bible I read: 'For your immortal Spirit is in all things' (Wis 12:1). O Holy and living Trinity! I was beside myself for a few days and that experience is still strongly impressed in my mind today.[2]

I have heard others tell of very similar experiences. You see, we have been created to enter into the love that eternally flows between the Father and the Son, to be caught up into that love which resides and pulsates within the Godhead itself. So when God said, "It is not good for the man to be alone," I realised that Adam was the picture of the much greater and eternal reality in which the Father said to the Son, "It is not good for You to be alone. To really bless You,

---

2   Raniero Cantalamessa, *Life in Christ: a Spiritual Commentary on the Letter to the Romans*, (The Liturgical Press, 1990).

I will create a helper for You, a Bride for You, as Your counterpart!"

The account in Genesis says that God brought all the animals in front of Adam for him to name them, but for Adam, "no suitable helper was found." The Old Testament is full of these prophetic pictures that speak about a greater reality revealed in the New Covenant. These pictures and symbols point to the superior spiritual realities found in the New Covenant.

Here in this second chapter of Genesis we have a clear prophetic picture. It is a picture of the 'birth' (if I may use that terminology) of Eve. If Jesus is the 'second Adam', then the Church *must* be the 'second Eve'. Here, in Genesis 2, we have the picture of how the Church was formed out of the side of Jesus. The Lord God caused the man to fall into a deep sleep. This correlates to Jesus' death on the cross, out of which the Father brought forth the Church from His side. It is interesting to note that the word 'rib' is not in the original Hebrew. The original language renders more accurately that God took the woman *from the side* of the man, creating her from what was taken from the man's side. When you read it like this you cannot help make the connection with the piercing of Jesus' side by the Roman soldier and the gushing out of blood and water. The Church was born by redemption and by the outpouring of the Spirit.

When the man saw his wife he exclaimed, "This is now bone of my bones and flesh of my flesh..." I find this very interesting. When Jesus appeared to His disciples after rising from the dead He used a similar expression, *"Touch me and see. A spirit does not have flesh and bones as you see I have."* (Luk 24:36-40) Interestingly, He does not speak of 'flesh and blood' because He had poured out His blood on the cross. The language 'flesh and bones' speaks prophetically of what was to come: the Church taken out of Jesus' side to be His helper. Watchman Nee, in his book *The Glorious Church,* expands on this. He states, "Only that which is out of Christ can be the Church." He expands this thought to come to the amazing conclusion that the Church "...is made from Christ Himself...The Church is another form of Christ just as Eve was another form of Adam."[3]

When God originally created the man and then the woman, they were one. The image of God was in man and woman together – masculinity and femininity in synergy – so much so that they were both known as *adam* (Gen 5:1,2). They only had one name because they were one. It was as if there was one being in two parts, rather than two separate beings. It wasn't until after the Fall that Scripture records Adam naming his wife, Eve (Gen 3:20). They no longer shared the same unity that they had when God originally created them.

We are the gift of love between the Trinity. The heart of the Son in eternity was to bring many sons and daughters home to His Father. The heart of the Father was to form a Bride for His Son, of the selfsame substance as the Son. The Bride is made up of the many sons and daughters. In Christ, what was divided through the Fall has been reunited again. The Church is the body of Christ now, and is separate from her Husband, but a day is coming when the Father will present her complete to His Son and she will become fully united with Him. In that day, the Father's family will be complete, at home with Him. We will be in the full interchange of the love that exists within the Trinity itself.

---

3   Nee, Watchman. *The Glorious Church: God's View Concerning the Church,* (Living Stream Ministry, 1993).

5 | The Mother Heart of God

"Comfort, comfort ye, My people," says your God.
Isa 40:1

I remember going through a time in my life when I cried out to God, "If only You were a mother!" I was a young Christian, trying to sort my life out, and struggling with the idea of God as Father. It gave me no sense of security at all. My father had left the family; my mother was the one who stayed. What I knew was that a mother would never leave you. I desperately wanted to know that God had a tender side that I could trust, that He had something of a mother's love in Him. I wanted God to be able to identify with me as a woman.

Later, as James and I travelled around speaking about the love of God the Father and the way our relationship with our own fathers affects the way that we see God, many people would come up to us afterwards and say, "I didn't really have a problem with my father; my problem was with my mother." Or they would say they had difficulty opening up their hearts to a masculine figure.

Because there has been a war against the feminine, it follows that there has been a wholesale devaluing of women. Women are the ones who have the capacity to express the mother heart and the femininity of God the Father. As I said earlier, if I was the serpent and I wanted to destroy the human race, the obvious one to target was the woman. This is because it is through the woman that the tender side of the Father is expressed most fully. Without that tenderness, without that nurturing ability, the human race does not come into the image of God because it is *her* love – the love of a mother – that is the *foundational* love that God always intended us to receive.

We hear a lot these days about 'a fatherless generation' and, indeed, we can look at the world and see that it definitely is a fatherless generation. But the reality is, if you have a fatherless generation, then you may also have a *motherless* generation. Because the mothers have to rise up in their masculine strength, in doing so they can lose the ability to nurture their young in the way that children need to be nurtured.[1]

Sadly, the most dispensable part of our humanity, particularly in our Western culture, is the quality of tenderness and nurture. In our culture it is masculinity and its related characteristics that are valued and attained to. Characteristics such as productivity and individuality, for example, are held up as high ideals within our society. When we are living in that kind of performance-driven culture the easiest thing to lay aside is the emotion and practice of tenderness. I remember going through hard times and difficulties when I was growing up, and, while my heart may have been screaming out, "That really hurt," I simply shut that emotion down and did not let anyone see my weakness. The result is that the tenderness and the ability to nurture is what gets

---

1   Jean Vanier in his book, *Man and Woman He Made Them* (St. Paul Publications, 1985) speaks of 'the wounded heart' of a child, "Between the baby and its parents, there is a life-giving dialogue which stimulates, calls forth, encourages and supports. The tiniest baby senses whether or not it is truly precious to parents, loved by them in a unique way."

pushed down. The reality is that God put within us the uniqueness as a mother, the uniqueness of the feminine, and the capacity to nurture.

I always think of it like this: it is the mother, or feminine love, who puts the heart into the human race. She is the one who teaches us how to love. A mother that is whole enough within herself is the one who teaches her children how to both love and be loved. As a mother is operative enough in herself to be able to love and nurture her infant she puts within that child the ability to receive and contain love – a container that can overflow to others. As human beings we have to be taught everything. We have to be taught how to walk, how to talk and how to eat among many other things. But we also need to be taught *how to love*. The Bible makes this clear when it says that we only love because God first loved us (1 Jo 4.19).

Love is a response to love. We learn how to love as a response to being loved. In contemporary culture there are many, many children who have missed out on this. The enemy has come to destroy our ability to love, and the more that this is happening, the more dangerous the world is becoming. The apostle Paul said,

> *This know also, that in the last days perilous times shall come. For men shall be lovers of their own selves... without natural affection ...lovers of pleasures more than lovers of God* (2Ti 3:1-4 (KJV).

This is really what is happening now. We are increasingly coming into a time when the ability to nurture is being lost. Motherhood is often valued less than being a 'career-woman', than doing your own thing, having your own business, etc. One of the major ambitions of many young women today is to make their way in the corporate world. I have no doubt that women are capable of balancing both a career and a family, but the need for tenderness and nurture needs to be valued and given high priority.

This applies to men also. Because males are not being nurtured, they in turn are unable to nurture their wives and their children. As a result, women are finding themselves more and more in a position where they are forced to go it alone and look after themselves and their families. In doing so, their ability to nurture and raise healthy offspring is jeopardized. If we look at many places around the world known as 'trouble spots' we find that women there are largely un-affirmed and undervalued. There is a principle of cause and effect at work here. Women who are undervalued are less able to nurture. The repression of true femininity stifles the nurturing instinct. Offspring within this context have no empathy for others; the young fail to understand how it feels to be tormented and so are much more prone to dispense it.

We can only learn by what is done to us. We are es-sentially receivers. Jesus said, "Freely you have received, freely give" (Mat 10:8). This is manifested both positively and negatively. Children, who have received love and ten-derness in their upbringing, will in turn be able to express love in a healthy way. In the same way, children who have received violence and neglect in their upbringing will give out violence and neglect to others. It takes an amazing move of the Spirit of God to heal some of the traumas that people have been through so that they can become loving and whole human beings.

I cannot separate this truth about motherhood and femininity from the bigger picture that God had in mind in creating us (both male and female) as a bride for His son. As well as being the Bride of Christ, I believe that we are to display the femininity and the nurturing heart of God on the earth. We are not only the Bride, however. Adam named his wife Eve, which means "the mother of all living." This is significant because as Adam is a type or shadow of Christ, so Eve is also a type and shadow of the Church. As Jesus was the second Adam, the Church is the 'second Eve' – the mother of all living. God's intention then is that she, the Church, would become the nurturing body on earth. His purpose was that the Church would incarnate His nurture. Through the Church, God Himself would be able to pour His love and tenderness, His grace and mercy, to a world that is broken and needy. This is, on a grander scale, what the mother is in the home. What the mother is within the home, so the Church is to be in the world.

We can see why the enemy has orchestrated a meticulously well-planned attack on the feminine image, so that a mother could not be what God intended for her to be in the home, unable to nurture and bring her children into the full image of God. When the feminine is devalued, the Church is unable to really nurture the broken world around it, until God comes and does this healing. I believe that God wants the Church to be His arms, and be His embrace to the world. His arms, His legs, His eyes, His ears, His mouthpiece, the Church is to be the incarnation of Him, the God of love. We have done very well in some aspects of this such as going to the nations, preaching the gospel, and baptising new disciples. We, the body of Christ, have been relatively good at going. What we are not so good at yet, is being!

We have yet to learn to just be the mother in the house of this world. We need to have tender hearts and open arms in synchronicity with the Bridegroom and with the Father Himself. His desire is to pour and express His love through the Bride and through the Mother that is on the earth.[2]

---

2   The concept of the mother heart of God is not unknown in Church history. Indeed, many of the Fathers as well as later theologians used feminine imagery

From the point of conception to when we entered the world, God intended that we should receive a specific kind of love, a specific quality of love so that we would grow up to be like Him. That quality of love is what He has put within a mother primarily, a mother who is whole enough within herself to express it. It is known in Greek as *storge*.[3]

This particular kind of love is separate from other kinds of love. It is the word for 'family affection'. It conveys the idea of nurturing, tenderness and care. *Storge* love is the type of love that builds the foundation of our life. It primarily comes from the mother because we grow within her womb and are comforted and nourished by her body from the birth onwards. However, it also comes from the father. Someone told me once that the word 'husband' has its roots in the old English word 'house-binder' which conveys the thought of overshadowing and protecting. A father can show affection

---

in their writings. Here are some examples:

Irenaeus (AD. 130-202), " ... He ... offered Himself to us as milk [because we were] as infants."

Clement of Alexandria (AD 150-230), " ... flee to the Word, the care-soothing breast of the Father, who alone, as is befitting, supplies us children with the milk of love," and, " ... the Father's breasts of love supply milk."

John 'Golden Mouth' Chrysostom (AD 354-407) so nicknamed because of his oratorical preaching, in a doxology speaks of Christ as, " ... brother, bridegroom, dwelling place, food, raiment, root, foundation ... sister, mother."

The apologists (Justin, Tatian, Athenagorus and Theophilus of Antioch make reference to the Word living in womb of God, like the embryo in the mother's womb.

Clement, again, " ... and while the unspeakable part of Him is Father, the part that has sympathy with us is Mother."

The above quotes are referenced from research by Dr. Tim Bulkeley of Carey Baptist College, Auckland.

Another notable comment is by the Reformer, John Calvin, who wrote in his commentary on Isaiah that, "God has manifested Himself to be both Father and Mother so that we might be more aware of God's constant presence and willingness to assist us."

3 For a more complete understanding of the Greek definitions for love see C. S. Lewis's book, *The Four Loves, Reprint Edition* (Fount, 1998).

to his offspring by surrounding and protecting the household, keeping it secure and free from fear and anxiety. *Storge* love is also conveyed through the wider family, through siblings, grandparents, and beyond.

The truth is that God intended our first experiences of this life to be (in the words of Paul the apostle) "rooted and grounded in love." We are meant, from the very beginning, to be rooted and established in this *storge* type of love. He intended that we would be loved with this quality of affection in abundance from our mother's womb and from the time we entered this world. It is only when the roots of our life go down deeply into the soil of love, and importantly, into the *right kind* of love, that we can grow up to be whole human beings and able to fully express the love that is in the heart of the Father for the world. God intended for us to experience that quality and quantity of love. When we first came into the world His intention was that we would be immediately initiated into that familial affection and tender love expressed personally through our mothers.

We are *made* for love. The person who is loved the most in the right kind of way is usually the most confident person, the one who is able to take the most knocks in life, able to suffer setbacks and to respond in the most healthy way. Often the person who has excelled academically does so because they have an inner quietness and confidence deep in the very centre of their being where they are able to rest and receive. God intended that we all would come into a place like that so that we could grow up into His image. And so, He put within the heart of the feminine – the feminine that is within *both* the man and the woman – the tender longings and the tender heart of Himself. It is important to recognise that men also have the ability within themselves to express these tender longings that come from the femininity of God.

In saying that, however, there is a way in which *more* of God's femininity resides within the female body. The female body is made for nurture. The female body is a prophetic expression of who God is in His feminine attributes. It is so significant that God revealed Himself (Gen 17:1) as El Shaddai, the Many Breasted One.[4] His purpose was that the nations (coming from Abraham whose name means "father of many nations") would be founded in love and in nurture. That was the revelation that Abraham had – El Shaddai, the Many Breasted One.

There is something about the breasts that speaks of comfort and nurture. We know that, in one sense, God does not have a body. He is spirit. But there is something in the way that He has formed us as human beings that gives a revelation of what His character is like and what His desire is for us as individuals within a home and a family, and also in the Church. I believe that He wants to express, through the Church, His nurture – to have the Church as the incarnation of the nurturing breasts of God.

A dear friend of mine who intercedes for me had a revelation one day. She said, "Denise, the Lord wants us as the body of Christ to love with breast milk, to feed with breast milk – not formula." Now that is very interesting! What she is saying is that the Church needs to be able to nurture from the substance of love within it and to bring that nurture to the world. If the church doesn't have breasts it can only minister through formulas! Why? Because God's love and His nurture comes through the breasts! The default to using formulas in many churches today only goes to illustrate that there is no organic nurture coming from the breasts. The

---

4   This has been rendered as 'The All-Sufficient One' but the word '*shad*' in Hebrew means 'breast' and added to El (a name for God) means 'God – the Breasted One.'

Church is meant to nurture with the life-giving milk that comes from the Father Himself.

Scripture itself speaks of the "milk of the Word" (1Pe 2:2 (NASB):

> *Like newborn babies, long for the pure milk of the Word, so that by it you may grow in respect to your salvation, if you have tasted the kindness of the Lord.*

Then, Paul writes: 1Co 3:1,2:

> *Brothers, I could not address you as spiritual but ... as mere infants in Christ. I gave you milk, not solid food, for you were not yet ready for it.*

These verses paint a picture of a mother who is nursing her infant child, feeding it with milk from her breast. This is a very deliberate picture conveyed in these verses by the Holy Spirit, for He wants to first of all nourish His people (the Church), and then nourish *through* His body (the Church) as a mother nurses her infant with nourishing milk. As I have pointed out, even our bodies are a revelation of who God the Father is! A mother is made for tenderness to incarnate the tender affection of God our Father.

This is not a popular truth for much of feminist thinking. You cannot get away from it however. A woman's body is made for nurture. It is made for tenderness. I am not saying that this is the limit of what a woman can do; of course, there is much more that a woman can do. Neither am I saying that she has to be confined there but the point I am wishing to emphasise is this: What we are finding in contemporary culture is an outright rejection of this reality and a denial of the fact that a woman's body is designed for nurture. So we find that we are departing more and more from the image of God.

Some time ago, I was staying with my daughter who lives with her husband and children in Sydney, Australia. I read in a news report that there is growing resentment among some members of society who are not happy about the tax benefits given to those with children. Another issue was people demanding the right to a seat on planes or restaurants that have 'child-free' areas.[5] Here are just two examples of how far away from the image of God we are becoming. This is a frightening reality because it is the mothers who put the heart into the human race. It is through her ability to love and nurture that we, in turn, receive and possess the ability to love and nurture. A mother is totally responsive to her child. It is a scientific fact that the brain of a woman is far more receptive to empathetic sadness than that of the man.[6] That is why it is usually the mother who gets up to a crying baby in the middle of the night; her senses respond to sadness if she senses that her baby is in distress and she *has to* respond to it. God has put something within us as mothers, which needs to respond to our children.

Sadly, I find that the Church is moving in a similar direction to contemporary Western culture, moving away from the desire and the ability to nurture. The world, however, is hungry for a mother's embrace. There is an Indian lady, universally known as Amma (Mother) who spends all of her time travelling throughout the world, holding events that are attended by thousands of men and women. She spends time giving each individual person a maternal embrace. Businessmen in expensive suits fall on her shoulder weeping. They queue for hours just to be told, "My darling son" and

---

5   Report by Sally Loane in *The Sydney Morning Herald*, 10 July 2000 entitled Two's all the company you want in the childfree zone. This was commenting on a book by Susan and David Moore, *Child-Free Zone: Why More People are Choosing Not to be Parents*, Checkered Gecko Pty.Ltd., NSW, 2000.

6   Research by Professor Simon Baron-Cohen of the Autism Research Centre, Cambridge University as reported in the BBC's Science and Nature web page.

be hugged by her. Women cannot restrain themselves from weeping when they hear the words, "My precious daughter" as they are enfolded in Amma's embrace, and have a candy or a petal pressed into their palm.

Females have a God-given capacity and calling, whether single or married, to impart something of the nurturing heart of the Father. This is a much bigger issue than natural mothering of children. It is about embracing who God has created us to be so that we incarnate His nature. Love responds to love. People will invariably respond to tender love. God has called the Church to minister to a broken world. The United Nations has recently speculated that the numbers of street children in the world today is in the tens of millions and may even be as much as 100 million.[7] That is a shocking statistic! Never before in history has there been such a big problem as there is today. The rise in the numbers of children living rough is symptomatic of the breakdown in society of the ability and willingness to nurture. These children do not have a home or a place to belong.

Given this, what then is God calling the Church to be? There is a tremendous need in the world in this area alone – with children who have never known what it is to be loved and nurtured.

I remember reading a newspaper article when we were in England some years ago. It was an article about 'child killers' – children under 15 years of age who had killed another person and who were incarcerated because they were killers. The newspaper had devoted an entire page to photographs of these children. The article went on to say

---

7   UNICEF, 2002:37. This figure varies according to interpretation as to whether it is the actual numbers growing globally or just that awareness is increasing. Nevertheless, a very conservative estimate of street children is at least in the tens of millions.

that studies done on the children concluded that the missing link was nurture within the early months and years of their lives. Even though some had come from apparently very well to do and stable homes, the bottom line was that they had not received the nurture needed to develop the part of the brain that specifically identifies with the pain and suffering in others. The lack of nurture was closely related to a resulting lack of empathy. This only goes to highlight the departure from God's desire for everyone who was ever born to have a mother who was able to dispense this nurturing love.

There is something that God has put within the feminine that a baby really responds to – the softness of the feminine. When a father holds a baby he gives to the baby a whole different impartation to what a mother gives. The baby feels the strength of his arms, the solidity of his chest, the safety and definition within the man. What the father gives is meant to convey the sense of a defined world out there, a feeling of the essential 'other'.

But when a mother holds a baby, the baby feels gentleness and tenderness, that 'sinking into' feeling, which is a feeling of oneness. This is the oneness that we are born to feel. We were never meant to feel alone. God never created us as humans to ever feel that we are on our own. The most traumatic experience a child can have is to be abandoned. The feeling of abandonment – whether real or imagined – is the worst thing a child can experience. Sometimes a person can feel abandoned even when they are totally loved. For example, if a child has an illness in early infancy and has to be hospitalised, then the mother may be breaking her heart with the pain of separation from the child – but the child will still feel abandoned. The subjective experience of the child (and the related emotions) is that of abandonment. The enemy comes in and emphasises that feeling, to perpetuate the lie that they have actually been abandoned.

The most traumatic thing that a human being can experience is that separation from bonding. This can be the basis for both mental and physical illness. We were never made to be alone. God always intended that we would be deeply connected and know the bonds of that connectedness. The primary bond, of course, is the bond to our mothers. We come from her body. Scientists are increasingly discovering how much input a baby can receive in the womb, and how much the mother's emotions (both negative and positive) are transmitted to the baby within her womb.

It is wonderful the way that God has made us. Did you know that when a baby is born all it can see is the distance from the mother's breast to the mother's eyes? That is the extent of the focus of the baby's eyes – the distance from the mother's breast to her eyes! Isn't that remarkable! There is something about the gaze of a mother as she looks at her newborn babe. It is wonderful to see the transformation of a young couple from being 'two' to being 'three,' and observe a young woman who is having her first baby. She can be nine months pregnant and quite composed yet the moment she has become a mother she is transformed! There is a maternal look now on her face and it is plain to see that she has become a mother. A transformation happens in a young woman who is emotionally whole enough to really receive that child. A newborn infant can receive the loving gaze of its mother. There is a way in which a mother looks at her baby that is flooded with affection and love. You have to witness it to understand what it is, the look that is so filled with unbridled love and affection for that child.

Even now we find that when a mother's milk is released a hormone is released with it and this brings and enhances maternal feelings. When I had my first baby I was the only mother in the entire hospital who was breastfeeding my child. I know that the trend has now swung back towards breastfeeding but at that time it was actually considered an unhealthy habit (that is what one of the nurses said to me!) so they would bind up the breasts of women to stop the milk coming. They would administer medication and take all kinds of measures just to stem the flow of milk from the mother's breasts. To me, that is indicative of this whole strategy to stop nurture from coming into the human race. It may sound as if I am on a particular bandwagon but when you see the whole picture you can see that the enemy is against humanity receiving nurture. The love that is humanity's inheritance comes (at least initially and foundationally) through the mother.

When I would get up in the middle of the night to breastfeed our children there was something intimate and wonderful about those night-time feeds when it was just the two of us – the baby and me. The baby was lying there, drinking and looking me right in the eye. The intimacy of eye-to-eye communication is at its height in these times.

The Bible says that the eye is the lamp of the body – through it we can see right into the human soul (Mat 6:22-23, Luk 11:34). When a mother gazes at her child and looks into the eyes of her baby with a smile of admiration, something is transmitted deep into the heart of that little child. Something that says, "You are welcome. You are mine. You belong." Whether it is communicated verbally or non-verbally – through the eye, the voice or through touch – the baby begins to learn something really important. They begin to realise at a primordial level that they are here in a place where they are welcome. Deeper than concepts or words the baby knows, "I am supposed to be here. I belong here."

One of the tremendous needs that we as human beings have is to feel that deep sense of belonging – that this is where I, as an individual, am supposed to be that this is my true home. It is a mother who first gives us that feeling of the essence of belonging. She does this through her gaze and she communicates the deep welcome verbally – through words, through the tone of her voice and the cadence of her speech.

There is a unique quality about a mother's voice. A baby cannot understand at an intellectual level what the words are but it comprehends at a much deeper level. Its spirit knows! Our human spirit has an antenna that picks up the essential and underlying meaning of the words that are spoken to us.[8] Jesus knew this when He said, "My words are spirit and they are life "(Joh 6.63). There is something in our human spirit that hears and understands what is being spoken. It can bring us into life or, conversely, the words of the enemy are spirit and death. Words carry the power of life and death, as Proverbs 18:21 says, "The tongue has the power of life and death, and those who love it will eat its fruit."

When a mother is communicating with her child through her voice, something is conveyed into the heart and into the life of that little child. The child becomes increasingly familiar with her voice, the vibrations of which resound within the womb. When children have been awoken during the night because they are afraid, maybe due to a bad dream, they love it when their mother slips into the bedroom and holds them, humming a soothing tune. Lullabies are intrinsically connected to the sound of the mother's voice,

---

8   Dr Paul Tournier citing scientific experiments writes, "[it is] ... an obvious fact ... that the foetus, at least in the later months of intra-uterine life, can hear his mother's voice.... Yes, you expectant mothers, your unborn baby can hear your voice. He can also hear the beating of your heart and the rhythm of your breathing. He is registering it all forever in his still unconscious mind. The perfect love that existed between mother and child during pregnancy was much more than a feeling, much more than an affective phenomenon. It was a communion of persons.". Paul Tournier, *What's in a Name?* (SCM Press Ltd., 1975).

bringing soothing reassurance to the heart of a child. Right from conception the child has heard the mother's voice. The resonance of her voice penetrates to the very ground of the child's being – to the foundations of its life. God has intended that we would hear the sound of the mother's voice, and receive her words as words of life – words to soothe and to comfort.

God says, "Comfort ye, comfort ye, My people!" (Isa 40.1). His words are tender. His deep desire is to bring words of comfort and tenderness. The tender sounds of the mother's voice penetrate right to the heart of the one who is founded in her love and nurture. Paul understood this when he wrote to the believers in Ephesus, praying that the roots of their lives (both individual and corporate) would "go down into love" (Eph 3:17 NLT). That has not happened for many of us through our own natural conception, birth and infancy but the wonderful reality is that God the Father can come and He can root and establish us in His love. Why? Because we come from Him. We came *through* our mothers but we *originated* in Him.

You and I were conceived in His heart long before we were conceived in our mothers' wombs. He is the very source of our life. We can trace our origins back even further than our own natural conception and meet God in that place of original love. We can meet Him at the fountainhead of all belonging. He, the Source, can come to us and minister that primordial nurture that our hearts so desperately need.

In our ministry, we have seen wonderful miracles of healing in the lives of different people as God the Father has come – as a mother – and touched deep in the human spirit. He has come and ministered to the very foundation of human life, the very ground of being. He will come and not only be a father to you, but He will come and mother you.

We grow up with a deep need for this kind of love. It is not just a matter of wishing it be great if I could get it. No. The degree to which you have received the nurturing love is the degree to which you are an emotionally whole human being. Conversely, the degree to which you have *not* received this is the degree to which you need Father to come and pour His comforting love in to your heart. The Father *will* come and lay that foundation so that the roots of your life go down into the ground of unconditional love.

When the roots of our psyche do not go deeply into love, there will be negative results in our lives. I believe that this is the reason for much of the anger, hostility, insecurity and depression that is so prevalent in our culture today. There is an emptiness because there is no rich soil of nurturing love within the psyche of the individual. James and I have lived in Christian communities that were also ministry centres, as well as having many people share our home with us, through the years. Many of these people have said to us that they feel as if they are standing on the edge of a black hole, an abyss, into which they could fall in and descend forever into the darkness with no hope of escape. After talking to thousands of people who feel like this, I really believe that they are describing a vacuum in which there has been an absence of nurture. As a result, there is no sense of safety and security in the very ground of their human psyche. They have no idea whether or not they are going to make it in life, but stumble through it putting on an act and trying to be strong. They have no sense of their own unique identity on the inside. Nothing comes from the heart because the heart is completely shut down or may never have been awakened.

Feminine love is the only love that can give us the foundation that we need. I repeat what I have said previously, when the feminine has been devalued and destroyed, and is thus unable to nurture, there are huge repercussions within our culture and society. The feminine was meant to be the very source of life. Eve was named as the mother of all living. So often, however, because of brokenness, you could almost say that the feminine has become the mother of all death! We may come through her into physical life but sometimes into emotional death.

That may seem to be a shocking statement, but the reality is that many people have experienced – contrary to what should have been – that their mother has effectively acted as the child in the relationship, and has sucked the life out of them. People in this situation have felt, from infancy, a responsibility to look after and 'nurture' their own mothers. They have consequently grown up with a huge vacuum. Where they should have been nurtured, they have been forced to become the nurturer. They have been expected to draw from an empty well. With a tremendously overemphasized sense of responsibility, they feel as if they are responsible for the entire world! I have conversed with young women so lacking in nurture in life that they want to have a baby, so that they will have someone who, as they put it, will "love me unconditionally!" Many young women have, tragically, had children for this reason and the child is conceived and born out of such a broken expression of humanity. The ordained and natural order is reversed – the child becomes the parent!

Many men grow up feeling an inexorable pull towards women, and yet at the same time they have an inner voice crying, "Get me out of here!" There is a huge desire and need to be loved and nurtured but, on the other hand, the neediness is so great that they have never been able to fulfill their own mother's needs, wishes or hopes. Men and women have grown up in that kind of situation where the neediness of their own mother has sucked everything from them. As a consequence of this, both men and women then run towards women to meet their deep need but their satisfaction cannot be attained in a way that is pure and holy. Pornography, in reality, is just a 'little boy' or a 'little girl' acting out a need for tenderness and softness. They do not realise it but pornography is an extremely broken and damaged expression of that need which destroys rather than heals. The pornographic images promise much but all that they can actually deliver is more pain, more brokenness and more shame.

Even in churches there are many people who are caught in this kind of dilemma – running from women on the one hand, but on the other they are so needy for feminine connection. There are many men who try and get all of their 'mother needs' met through their wife's body. So many women have told me, "I feel like I am just like his mother. It is not about him and me in our marriage relationship. It is about him and his mother." She is not being loved by a bridegroom, but rather a little boy with infantile needs, expressing themselves in a mature male body. It all manifests in the marriage bed, so she closes down emotionally and sexually, and he feels more rejected and begins to seek other ways to satisfy his need. This pattern is very prevalent and my heart breaks over it. When we were pastoring, sometimes I would stand in front of our church congregation and I could see what was really happening on the inside of the people, good people who loved God, and who were trying to live a pure and holy life. They had continually repented of things such as lust, and yet both men and women were being drawn by something much deeper than their own understanding. They thought that they were intrinsically bad, beyond help, yet their problem was foundational in its nature. The reality was that the roots of their lives had not gone down into a pure and holy love that God intended them to have.

God is coming to reveal Himself, not only as Father – but also as 'Mother'. He can reveal Himself as 'the Breasted

One' – the One to whom you can come and receive nurture. You can receive nurture that is not going to destroy you but rather build you up in life. His feminine love will establish you to live in holiness because now you can have a source of intimacy and belonging.

King David, the shepherd-king of Israel, knew what it was to avail himself of the nurture of El Shaddai. In Psalm 131, burdened with the awesome responsibilities of military command and nation-building, he says,

> *My heart is not proud, O Lord, my eyes are not haughty; I do not concern myself with great matters or things too wonderful for me. But I have stilled and quieted my soul; like a weaned child with its mother, like a weaned child is my soul within me.*

He speaks here of himself as a child at the breast of its mother. Israel's greatest king sees himself in this way. He does not speak of being 'weaned' in the sense of being weaned off the breast in order to eat solid food. The word 'weaned' in this context carries with it the sense of a child being fully sated, engorged with its mother's milk, so that it lies milk-drunk and sleepy on the breast. Picture this king with the heavy burdens of statecraft laid down, and satiated at the breast of El Shaddai.

One of the ways that we learn intimacy and holiness together is as we are being fed at our mother's breast. There is something about it that is so intimate and yet so holy. In that experience there is the weaving together of intimacy and holiness. If we do not receive that, and are not rooted and established in that depth of love, we will always and ever be searching for it. We will never, ever be satisfied with anything else. We will continually be on a quest for it. Our romantic relationships may go some way towards assuaging it but there will always be a deeper need gnawing at our soul.

We have a constant need for Father – not only expressed in the masculine but expressed in the feminine. Thank God we can come to Him and receive an expression of His nurturing love. We can come to His breast and find intimacy and healing there. We can find deep bonding in that place.

In Isaiah 49:15 we read, "Can a mother forget the baby at her breast and have no compassion on the child she has borne? Though she may forget, I will not forget you!"

Here, God the Father is comparing Himself – not only to a mother but to a *nursing* mother.[9] He is comparing Himself to a mother whose milk has come down, who is engorged, where the oxytocin hormone has been stimulated, and who is expressing all the tenderness of a mother who is in 'full milk'. Here He is expressing the kind of love that will rise up one hundred times in the night for you, the kind of love that will even die for you. If you are crying from sickness or fear, this kind of love will always be available for you. This is the kind of love that knows no end. It will go on and on and on and on!

A mother's love will never stop. A mother who is connected to her maternal, God-given love will never cease to love, whatever the circumstances. There is no end to that quality of love. I remember hearing a story that illustrates this wonderfully. In the aftermath of a forest fire, workers were clearing the still-smoking ground and came across the charred carcass of a bird. As they moved the carcass aside, suddenly they saw a movement. Under the wings of the dead mother bird, her little fledglings were still alive - protected

---

9 Interestingly, John Calvin, the Reformed theologian, commented on this passage, " God did not satisfy Himself with proposing the example of a father, but in order to express his very strong affection, He chose to liken Himself to a mother, and calls His people not merely children, but the fruit of the womb, towards which there is usually a warmer affection." Quoted from his *Commentaries, Volume 8: Isaiah 33-66,* (Baker Books, 2005).

by their mother as the raging inferno passed over! She stayed there when she could have flown away to safety. She died rather than abandon her young. There is no end to the kind of love that a mother has. The love of a mother has no limits. It is very clear to me that this little story vividly conveys what God is like.

"Can a mother forget the baby at her breast and have no compassion on the child that she has borne?" With fallen motherhood it is actually possible that a mother is capable of forgetting and capable of lacking compassion. But He cries out, "Even though she may forget, I will not forget you!" He is a greater expression of motherhood than a human mother in the full flow of her nurturing. He is the original source and expression of motherhood. He is saying, "I have an infinitely greater capacity to comfort you and love you tenderly!"

Further on in this same prophecy, we see Jerusalem as a type and picture of the Church. It was God's intention that Jerusalem would be in the world what the Church is now to be in the world. God says, through the prophet,

> *Rejoice with Jerusalem and be glad for her, all you who love her; rejoice greatly with her, all you who mourn over her. For you will nurse and be satisfied at her comforting breasts; you will drink deeply and delight in her overflowing abundance.*

He is speaking prophetically about His love being shown through the Church:

> *For this is what the Lord says, "I will extend peace to her like a river, and the wealth of nations like a flooding stream; you will nurse and be carried on her arm and dandled on her knees.*
>
> *As a mother comforts her child, so will I comfort you; and you will be comforted over Jerusalem.*

Here it is!

As a mother comforts her child, so will I comfort you; and you will be comforted!

As a mother comforts her child! Isn't this amazing? The way that a mother comforts her child is different than the way that a father comforts his child. Mothers and fathers administer comfort in completely different ways. When a little child, for example, falls over in the garden and runs indoors crying with a grazed knee, the father – if he gets there first – will generally bend down, perhaps give the child a pat on the back and say, "You're O.K. Off you run and play. Everything will be fine!" That is the way that a father comforts and that is the right way for a father to comfort because it is a father's role to enable and strengthen.

A child, however, will generally attempt to run past Dad and get to Mum, because a mother comforts in a completely different way. A mother will stoop down and scoop the child into her arms. She will hold her child, soothe them and let them cry. She will comfort them.

God says, "You will be comforted at her comforting breasts, as a mother comforts – differently to a father – so will I comfort you!"

He is coming to us as the Church, the New Jerusalem, to comfort us in the same way that a mother comforts, with His comforting breasts, to extend peace to us like a river. One thing about a person who has not been nurtured is that they know no peace. There is something internal that cannot and will not rest; something continually in motion like the restless waves. Many people cannot stand silence. Silence intimidates them. They walk into the house and immediately turn on the television or the radio. They abhor the silence and want to fill it with lots of noise. An un-nurtured person finds it very difficult to rest and be still. God says, "If you come to this place, I will extend peace to you like a river – and I will comfort you as a mother comforts." It is a deep and universal need that we have. Not just to be loved by a father. It is not just a fatherless world. It is truly a motherless world. The world needs a mother, and we, the Church, are to be that mother.

6 | The Cloud of Love

I can see as my spirit discerns the future and reaches out to touch the heart of mankind and the desire of God, that there is coming from heaven a new manifestation of the Holy Spirit in power, and that new manifestation will be in sweetness, in love, in tenderness, and in the power of the Spirit, beyond anything your heart or mind ever saw. The very lightning of God will flash through men's souls. The sons of God will meet the sons of darkness and prevail. John G. Lake

Some years ago I had an experience in which it became very clear to me what the heart and purpose of the Father really is. Returning home to New Zealand after being in Europe ministering, I went through Sydney to visit my daughter, Amanda. While I was there I received an invitation to speak at a local church the following Sunday. Because I am a somewhat reluctant speaker my husband, James, has always given me a little piece of advice. He said to me, "Whenever you receive an invitation to speak, immediately say, 'Yes' without thinking about it, because if you think too much about it first you will never agree to speak anywhere." So, after wavering momentarily, I agreed to preach the following Sunday. I had a full week to seek the Lord and receive a message to speak to the church.

I was having difficulty sleeping because of jet lag and one night I woke up in the early hours of the morning, about 2 a.m. As soon as I woke up I had an immediate awareness that the entire room was absolutely filled with the tangible presence of God. It would not be an exaggeration to say that it was one of the most potent experiences of God's presence that I have ever had. If the Lord had been manifested physically before my eyes it would not have been any more real than what I experienced that night. The air was electric with His presence. I felt as if every single cell of my body was loaded and charged with the living Word of God. In that moment I felt as if I had come into all knowledge, that all things were revealed to me and that I knew all mysteries. I felt as if I could have named the countless stars in many galaxies. As Adam named the animals and that is how they were subsequently known, I knew then that God had truly purposed to give dominion to mankind. God had trusted Adam and, in that experience, I knew what this was like. In His presence, nothing was hidden from me. All was revealed. I felt as if I knew many, many Scriptures without having to learn them, for they were there, resident within the centre of my being.

Fortunately or unfortunately – depending on how you view it – when the presence of the Lord departed, all of that knowledge departed with it. I was back to my normal self. After the experience passed, I was no more knowledgeable than I was before I went to bed that night. During that time however, what seemed to be fullness of knowledge was present with me.

There were some things, however, that God spoke to me which I did remember after His tangible presence lifted. One of them struck me greatly. He said with deep poignancy, *"I am laying a new foundation of love in My Church."* When I heard this, my immediate thought was, "This is Sunday's message! I've got it!" I didn't realise that it was a word to my own heart, first and foremost, but that it also had deep and far-reaching implications for the whole body of Christ.

A new foundation of love in My Church! As I pondered on this I recalled a quotation that I had read and written down in the flyleaf of my Bible. It was from John G. Lake, who was mightily used of God in signs and wonders, particularly in South Africa. Nearing the end of his life he made this statement:

> *I can see as my spirit discerns the future and reaches out to touch the heart of mankind and the desire of God, that there is coming from heaven a new manifestation of the Holy Spirit in power, and that new manifestation will be in sweetness, in love, in tenderness, and in the power of the Spirit, beyond anything your heart or mind ever saw. The very lightning of God will flash through men's souls. The sons of God will meet the sons of darkness and prevail.*

When I originally read that statement I was really impressed. This was a man who had witnessed God's power in remarkable ways. I thought that if I could just see what he saw, I would die a happy woman! He said that the new manifestation would be "in sweetness, in love [and] in tenderness" – something that your eyes or mine have never seen. What John G. Lake saw coming in the future would be greater than anything that he witnessed in his lifetime.

I began to ponder on all the manifestations of power that have been demonstrated through people such as John G. Lake, and through the great forerunners of church history who have become household names because of significant anointing in the miraculous. Incredible signs and wonders have been witnessed through their ministries, particularly in the last century, and yet this is something beyond that, something entirely different. John G. Lake saw a move of God in the future that would be infinitely greater than anything seen before and it would be marked with the qualities of sweetness, tenderness and love. I do not believe that we have seen signs, wonders, miracles and life-transformations that have come "in sweetness, in love and in tenderness." We have seen demonstrations of faith and of the working of power. We have even seen the anointing wielded in what might be termed a 'harsh' manner nevertheless it was of the Spirit and it worked. The methodology of a man like Smith Wigglesworth was very successful and undoubtedly it was in alignment with the Spirit, but you cannot exactly say that it was in sweetness, tenderness and love. The overall effect of it was somewhat different, coming in power and dynamism rather than sweetness and tenderness.

But friends, something different is coming! Different in essence, different in quality, different in *modus operandi.* Different than anything we have seen before, beyond anything that your heart or mine ever saw. When I was in the middle of this experience, in the night with the Lord, I could see all that. I could see that God is doing a new thing and it is coming in sweetness, tenderness and love.

The first time I ever spoke the message of the Father having a mother's heart, Jack Winter, who was our spiritual father and in whose ministry was the seedbed of our current ministry, made a very telling observation. He said, "I think what we are talking about, the experiencing of the Father's love, is *really* the outpouring of the Mother heart of God."

I really believe that! Why do I believe it? Because it is coming in a different way. Whether it comes through a man or a woman, whether we are specifically talking about God the Father or not, the real essence is His gentleness, His grace, His mercy, and His love. These attributes are normally asso-ciated with femininity. Generally the ministry of a father in our lives is to enable us, to envision us, to strengthen us to go out to places we have not been before, to be risk-takers. A father gives identity and masculine strength to go forth and bring about kingdom rule. A father says, "I believe in you. You can do it!"

God is beginning to put in place a new foundation, to pour His love into the foundations of the Church as it was in the beginning. I believe that it will surpass anything experienced in the history of the Church. We are at the beginning of the beginning of God revealing Himself as a father. He is a better father than we have ever dreamed of. He is a father who has all of the good masculinity to enable and strengthen us, to send us forth, but He is also a father who has a tender mother's love with understanding, compassion, mercy and comfort. These attributes are all in Him and He is beginning to manifest Himself thus in these days.

As I was thinking over what had occurred during that night, I was also anticipating preaching the following Sunday. I didn't really have a well-prepared message but I thought that I would simply stand up and tell the people about the love of God. The church I was to speak in was a very active church and full of purpose. They had a vision to reach Sydney, Australia, and beyond with the Gospel. They were a very mission-focused church. When I stood up that Sunday I began to talk about the love of God and about what the Father is really like. I talked about His love, His compassion, His mercy and goodness, His grace and tenderness.

Then something extraordinary happened. As I was speaking, I began to perceive what was like a mist coming into the building. It was billowing very softly through the walls at the back of the auditorium and it began to form into a cloud. The cloud was moving and expanding and beginning to fill up the whole room. I was really in the Spirit and I wasn't sure which eyes I was seeing it with. Was it my physical eyes or was I having a spiritual vision? It seemed so obvious and natural to me that I didn't think to ask anyone else whether or not they were also seeing this.

As the cloud moved up the room, strange things began to happen to the congregation. What began to happen was not normal in this church and was not expected. Some members of the congregation were sliding gently from their chairs onto the floor. Some were laughing, others were weeping. The whole congregation was under the weight of this cloud of divine presence that was moving through the room.

As I was looking at this cloud, I felt to say something. I wanted to say, "The Father is here" because I had been talking about His love. In my spirit, however, I did not feel a liberty to say that. Those were not the appropriate words to say. Then I thought to say, "Jesus is here," but somehow I could not get the words out. I could not even bring myself to say that it was the Holy Spirit. Finally, all that I was able to say was this: *"Love has come! Love is here!"* It was what I would call a full Trinitarian experience, where Father, Son and Spirit came to dwell. And, because God had come and God *is* love, then Love had come. When the Godhead comes to us, Love itself comes for God *is* love and that divine love was potently real at that time.

Then I began to experience something similar to what I had experienced that previous Thursday night. The Scriptures became intensely alive to me. Many things were beginning to happen throughout the congregation as the cloud was expanding and moving through the room. I found myself caught up in a flash of revelation. Ephesians 3:14-19 was being opened up to me. In these verse, the apostle Paul says:

> *For this reason I kneel before the Father, from whom His whole family in heaven and earth derives its name. I pray that out of His glorious riches He may strengthen*

> you with power through His Spirit in your inner being,
> so that Christ may dwell in your hearts through faith.
> And I pray that you, being rooted and established
> in love, may have power, together with all the saints,
> to grasp how wide and long and high and deep is the
> love of Christ, and to know this love that surpasses
> knowledge – that you may be filled to the measure of all
> the fulness of God.

What particularly struck me was this: we have to be *strengthened with power,* through the Spirit in our inner being, to encounter the fullness of God. We do not have the capacity within ourselves to be containers of the eternal love of God. Paul is praying here that our spirits will be strengthened so that we might really know in our hearts and spirits what this love is. This love is too big to be known by the human intellect. This love is too big for the mind as it surpasses knowledge. This love will blow your mind. But this love can be known when the Holy Spirit strengthens your inner being with power. The Greek word for 'know' here is *ginosko,* which carries with it the meaning of "becoming deeply acquainted with at a heart level" in the same way that a man has union with a woman. It carries the meaning of intimate knowledge. We need to be strengthened by the Spirit to *know (ginosko)* the love of God in the depth of our hearts. You get a sense that Paul is struggling with the confines of human language to express the full reality of his experience of the love of God.

The wonder of it all! To grasp how wide and long and high and deep is the love of Christ and to know this love! This, dear friend, is a heart knowing, a spiritual knowing. The knowledge that it surpasses is knowledge on the human, intellectual level. The human mind will never have any conception of the superlative capacity of the love of God. *This* love of God is too big for human comprehension. I believe that Paul was getting carried away in his spirit as he penned these words. I would recommend reading this passage over and over again and meditating upon it to begin to grasp the truth of what it is saying.

Paul prays that we would be strengthened, "out of His glorious riches." I was very familiar with the expression, "… the power of Your love." I had sung those words often in worship but it dawned on me that I hadn't a clue what it really meant! I had no idea what the power of His love actually is! Within ourselves we just *cannot* enter into it; neither can we even begin to contain it. He, through His divine Spirit, has to strengthen us to know and contain the might of His love.

To know from the heart – to experience His love is to experience a love that is infinitely greater than anything you or I can imagine. Wider than the expanse of the ocean, longer than the span of the earth, higher than the highest mountain, deeper than the deepest sea. It completely surpasses knowledge! We can *know about* love and we can experience it to a degree, but if you think of the best kind of love that you have ever experienced or have heard about on this earth, there is a limit to that kind of love. Love on this earth has a limit but *this* love has no limit. It is greater than anything our minds can conceive of. So many of us know about love but we have no experiential awareness of *the love* itself.

The reason we don't know the love of God is because we need to be filled with the Spirit to comprehend it and for it to be made real in our experience. We need to be filled with the Spirit because *He knows the love!* It is *His* knowing of the love that is made real to us in the depths of our being. The Holy Spirit can bring that knowledge to us because it is real to *Him* in the depths of *His* being – if I may use that language.

He has to strengthen us so that we might receive the love of God and then love with the love of God.

As this cloud was seeping in, another Scripture that became startlingly alive to me was 1 Corinthians 13, the well-known passage about love. This took me by surprise because, to be honest, this passage was pretty much devoid of any meaning for me. My priority in life was to get the job done, to achieve the goal. I had no time for love or no interest in the idea of love – how could I take time for loving when there was a world to be healed and saved? That was how I really felt! My prejudice about 1 Corinthians 13 was confirmed when I heard it read out as one of the chosen texts at the wedding of a friend. This friend was in the New Age movement and the use of that scripture at a New Age wedding confirmed absolutely to me my ambivalence about that particular passage. It was wishy-washy, meaningless and of no practical use. But…as I was watching this cloud of love come towards me, and witnessing what was unfolding as it moved through the congregation, I could see in my spirit the truth of 1 Corinthians 13. I saw that it was a revelation of what God *Himself* is really like.

Because God *is* love, this chapter is also a revelation of what God is like. In the previous chapter, Paul has been teaching about gifts and manifestations of the Spirit, about apostles, prophets and such things. But then he ends that section by saying, "…and now, I will show the most excellent way." This way, the way of love, is different to other ways of operating in the Spirit. You see, it is possible to operate in the things of the Spirit but yet be without love. When I thought about John G. Lake's words I knew that I had seen the gifts of the Spirit used, and used effectively, but not in sweetness, tenderness, and love. It was definitely of God, definitely anointed by the Spirit, gifts and ministries were in genuine operation but very often *without* love.

The truth is – faith *will* work. When we are moving in faith, faith *will* produce what it believes for. You can have a 'healing ministry'. You can have a 'miracle ministry'. You can even raise the dead – but it is by faith or anointing and not 'of love'. Paul says, "The only thing that counts is faith expressing itself through love" (Gal 5:6). We have seen much effectiveness in the ministry of the Spirit. James and I have seen a lot of things that have worked because we have had faith for it. I am the type of person who would have faced down doors of iron and commanded them to open before me, I would operate by my willpower and faith. But we have not seen the miraculous demonstrated in the sweet tenderness of love. Paul speaks of 'the most excellent way'. I believe that *this* is what God was talking about when He said to me, "I am laying a new foundation of love in My Church."

"If I speak with the tongues of men and of angels...*but have not love...*" Paul doesn't say, "If I don't do it in a nice or loving way," but rather he speaks of love as something that you have. He speaks of love as a substance which is possessed inwardly. If I *have not* love, I am nothing more than a resounding gong or a clanging cymbal.

"If I have the gift of prophecy and can fathom all mysteries and all knowledge." Think about that! What would I not give to be able to fathom *all* mysteries and all knowledge? I know a number of prophetic people who are extremely gifted and who have a high degree of accuracy in what they can hear from God. My tendency is to think that people like this are very close in relationship to God. But Paul says that it is actually possible to be like this, but without love it is nothing! Possessing the faith that is able to move mountains means nothing without love. Think about it; if you met someone who could have enough faith to see a mountain move into the sea, it would be impressive to say the least, *but without love it is nothing.*

Even something as radical as giving all I possess to the poor and surrendering my body to the flames means nothing without love. I do not think there would be many deaths harder to endure than to be burnt alive. There have been people who have gone as far as setting themselves on fire for a cause that they believe in, but without the substance of love, it profits absolutely nothing.

The apostle goes on to describe what love looks like. "Love is patient." Other versions say, "Love suffers long" (NKJV). I really love that rendition because I believe that it is as close to the true meaning as we can get. The love of a mother is a love that is able to suffer long. In fact, to her it is not suffering because she loves her child. When a mother sits up at night to comfort her child, in that sense she is not really suffering because her love for the child supercedes all suffering. For the onlooker who is seeing this from an objective viewpoint, it looks like the mother is suffering – but the mother is *not* suffering. She is *loving*. When Paul says, "Love suffers long," it is because it is about love rather than suffering. You see, love has a completely different perspective. The emphasis is not on suffering – *it is on loving.*

I could see all this within the cloud. The presence of God was so strong within that meeting. I knew beyond any doubt that love is the very antithesis of being self-seeking. I remember once having an experience where I was looking into the eyes of Jesus. Scripture says that God is a consuming fire (Heb 12:29). I have never feared that, because I know that the fire is an all-consuming love. During that experience, what really struck me about His eyes was that there wasn't one spark of self-interest in them. They were completely focused on the object of His attention – me. There was nothing in His gaze that could ever cast anyone away. As I looked into this cloud I could see that there is nothing that He requires of you. He requires nothing for Himself.

When He looks at you it is all about you. You absorb His attention fully. His disposition towards you is nothing but love, promise, compassion and hope. This love does not require you to do anything. It all flows in one direction.

This love that surpasses knowledge is a scandalous love. It keeps no record of wrongs. That is amazing. If you pause to really think about that statement it is scandalous. If you are focused on rules and regulations, on doing what is right and avoiding or even punishing that which is wrong this statement will be hard to swallow. A love that keeps no record of wrongs? I had a whole list of rights and wrongs, and the 'wrongs' were written in block capitals, underlined and in bold type! But *this* love keeps no record of them! Even if you ask for forgiveness for something you have done over and over, the Father in His love has no recollection of that. In His eyes, the first time you repented He forgave and then wiped out the record of it. This love is not the love that we are accustomed to. It supercedes every kind of love. It surpasses all knowledge.

One of the other things that was amazing was this. Within the cloud of love, divine knowledge was contained. When love came, everyone came into the light. The light of love exposed everyone's life. Within me I felt as if could have told each person the minute details of their lives. I sensed that, if I desired to, I could have accessed the knowledge and told them their mother's maiden name or where their grandfather was born. I felt as if that kind of information was easily and readily accessible within the atmosphere of love. The love itself contained all knowledge. Prophetic mysteries would be made known within this love. I knew what Paul meant when he proclaimed, "…then shall I know fully even as I am fully known" (1Co 13:12). It was a foretaste of heaven, to know fully and to be fully known. I felt that I knew the destinies of each person in the room, I could perceive the call of God upon their lives – untouched and unmarred by sin. I could see the reality of who God had created them to be as unique individuals, each one shining in beauty and splendour – without sin! That was how God viewed them. That was how Love Itself viewed them.

Many years later, I still meditate on what happened in that room, on that Sunday morning in a church in Sydney. Isn't it amazing that this Father does not see the things that drag us down? The world has a saying that "Love is blind" but the reality is that it is only love that truly sees. Love is not blind. It truly sees who its object *really* is. When you really love someone and they do something wrong, does it really matter? When you love them, the issue is not really what they have done. Any parent who really loves their child will know this. When the child does something wrong the love of the parent is not diminished. If that is true in our humanity, it is abundantly true for God. Take the love that a parent has for their child and multiply it over and over again to even begin to grasp what God's love is like. The love of God in Christ Jesus is far beyond our comprehension.

Invariably, when I speak of this in a conference or meeting, I always encounter the detractors who come up to me after I have finished. Those who eat from the tree of the knowledge of good and evil say, "Denise, but surely you are giving people license to sin! Surely people will take advantage of you telling them that God doesn't record their sins and go out and sin *more*!" I usually respond by telling them that I heard someone say if the preaching of the gospel does not lead people to ask "Can we continue to sin then?" then the gospel of grace has not really been preached. If people are not asking that question, you are not yet preaching the gospel of grace that Paul preached. Paul asks a rhetorical question, "What then? Shall we sin because we are not under law but under grace?"(Rom 6:15). He asks that because it is the question that follows logically from what he has been teaching about grace. He says then, "By no means!" But the whole point that he makes is that it is only grace and love that stops us sinning. The law empowers sin but grace and love removes its power. A friend of mine described it beautifully like this. She told me that in many of the large cattle ranches in Australia there are no fences – the land is so vast that it would be impossible to fence it. It is also very dry. But there are pockets of water here and there and the cattle never stray far away from the water. They don't need a fence because they will die of thirst if they stray away from the water. You see, there is no need for the law when our thirst is quenched in the pool of grace, in the river of love. There is freedom but it doesn't go beyond where this love will allow you to go. Love imposes its own limits out of consideration for the object of its affection. If we stray from the love of God, we get thirsty and then we are drawn back to drink deeply from that love again.

Love keeps calling you back. It draws you inexorably back into its centre and into its embrace. It always protects, always trusts, always hopes, always perseveres. This is what He is like. This passage is describing the love of the Father. This is amazing! We are often gripped by condemnation and feeling that we have let God down. Guess what? He still trusts us. He still perseveres in bringing us into the fullness of His purposes for our lives. He has boundless hope for us. He watches over us and protects us with tender care and with fierce strength.

This love never fails. The love that Paul is talking about in 1 Corinthians 13 is the same love that he talks about in Ephesians 3, where he prays that we might know the width and the length, the height and the depth of the love of Christ. This love is greater than our knowledge, but it is poured out in our hearts. This love can only be known in the heart because the knowledge of our heart has no boundaries. It is not contained by concepts, mindsets or regulations. The love of God is much bigger than that.

That day I realised that the New Covenant is all about love. I could see that anything in the New Testament that looked like a list of what to do or what not to do (and there are plenty of those statements particularly in Paul's letters) are actually *all about love*. The New Covenant is all about a revelation of the love of God for us. When Paul admonishes, for example, "Do not fornicate" or, "Do not get drunk with wine," the reason he is saying that is simply because to do those things you have to step out of love. Everything that Paul says that might be seen as prescriptive is related to God's family walking in love with one another. The whole point is to remain in love. I cannot gossip or talk negatively about you unless I step out of love. You cannot do those sorts of things and stay in the place of love. The goal of Christianity is that we learn how to live in love, grow in love, and learn how to drink it in until it becomes part of us. The Father's purpose for us is that we are swallowed up in His love and our relationships with one another cannot but be affected.

I have recently made a statement that may be construed as controversial but it is actually not. What I have said is this – The Father's love is too big for the Church. For some people that may sound quite radical but isn't that exactly what John 3:16 says? For God so loved the world! We have tried to contain and corral the love of God within the Church but we have not seen the big picture. We have not comprehended the Father's all-encompassing vision to see His love fill the entire created order. You see, we are all coming into our identity as sons and daughters. What is more than that, all creation is groaning and waiting for that manifestation (Rom 8:19, 20). God knew us long before our natural parents conceived us. He knew us when we were 'in Adam', as it were. He lost us through the Fall, but we were redeemed back to Him through the death of the Firstborn, His Beloved Son. Jesus came to bring us back into the love of the Father and to restore us to our destiny as sons and daughters.

The stunning truth of this hit me when I was in Hong Kong some years ago. I was speaking in a church on Sunday and the pastor asked me to come back during the week and address a group of refugees. So I went back to the church on Tuesday morning. The deal was that the refugees would come to the church building for a free lunch on the condition that they would sit through some Christian teaching. So, the lunch finished and the refugees filed into the adjoining room to hear what I would say. Most of them were men from Africa. A song was sung which the men did not participate in. My gifting is not really evangelistic and I didn't have a clue what I was going to say to these men. But, as the song finished and as I was about to get up to speak, the pastor leant across and whispered in my ear, "Did I mention that these men are all Muslims?"

My heart missed a beat. What had I got myself into? It took me completely by surprise. If I hadn't a clue what to say before, this realisation compounded my lack of readiness even more! All I could do was cry that prayer that comes directly from the heart – Help!

And He did. God *did* help me. As I was crying out very loudly on the inside, He said to me so quietly something that I never would have thought to say. He said, "Denise, just stand up and be a mother to them." I thought, "Okay. I can do that," so I stood up and I looked at these men. Few of them were older than our oldest son. So I said to them, "I haven't got a teaching for you but I just want to tell you what I would want you to know if I was your mother and you were my sons." So I began telling them about a Father who lives in heaven that loves them so much, that His desire for them was that they never would have experienced the kind of things they had lived through. They had been through the horrors of wars. Some of them had been child-soldiers and had made their escape from their masters. I told them how precious and beautiful they were in God's sight. As they looked at me I spoke to them from a mother's heart. Then I heard myself saying, "Now I am going to come down from the stage and stand at the front, and if any of you would like to be hugged by a mother, come to me. Many of you have never known what it is like to be tenderly embraced by a mother. Many of you have been given away, many of you have been taken away, and it may have been many, many years since you have seen your mother. But if you want a hug from a mother I am just going to wait here and be available."

I stood there and I waited and waited. Sometimes I caught their glance and nodded and smiled at them. Then, one by one, the braver ones came forward and I put my arms around them, and held onto them. When I hugged some of them I knew somehow that no-one had ever hugged them before. I could feel that they had gone through a lifetime having never experienced a mother's hug. Some held onto me so tight that it seemed that if they let go they might die. They were desperate for love and affection. As they came forward I told them how precious and lovable they were. I said, "You have never known how lovable you are but you are *really* lovable. There is such beauty and uniqueness in you." These men were some of the most hardened men I have ever met but I could see tears streaming down their faces.

Truly, that *was* the Father's love but He didn't require me in that instance to say, "Come to Christ." It was not about theology. It was about incarnation. He wanted me to demonstrate the reality of a Father who *so* loved the world that He gave of Himself. These were all His lost sons that He was reaching out to. Obviously, there was more for these men. Obviously, those who were ministering to them would tell them about the Son, Jesus, who gave His life to bring them to the Father. But that was not the first step. The first step is to know and experience the love itself. To be attracted by the love. This is the love that surpasses knowledge. This is the love that has no rules and boundaries. It is the love that comes from the Father Himself. It is His love for His children and His love for the world He created. All the families in the world get their name from the Father (Eph 3:15). Whether they know Him or don't know Him, He knows who they are. They may not know who He is, but His love *surpasses* knowledge and *He knows them*. This is the very thing that Jesus died for, that we might come to know this all-surpassing love.

My prayer for myself is that I would look upon people with the eyes of love. My desire is that I would see them from the perspective of the Tree of Life. That I would see them through the eyes of the Father. When Jesus was on this earth He broke so many rules that existed because of mere legalism. I love that about Him. For Jesus, the law of love was all-encompassing and superceded the petty rules that kept people in bondage. Likewise, King David, in order to feed his hungry troops, had the audacity to enter the Holy Place and avail himself of the consecrated shewbread for them to eat (1Sa 21:1-6). He had no compunction about handing the holy bread out to his friends. Jesus commends him for doing this (Mat 12:3-4). I exclaimed to James one day after reading this, "God loves it when we break the rules!" James responded, "I don't think that's what the Bible means." We laughed about it, but my point was that Jesus commended David for putting the welfare of his friends above the protocol of the temple. The text in Matthew 12 actually expands this point even more. Of course, James was making a valid point, but I am trying to emphasise this perspective. The law of love is the greatest principle in the universe. It sees things from a paradigm of relationship rather than barren functionality or mere dogma.

God is calling us into this love that changes everything. We can come to Him and walk in this love that surpasses knowledge. We can span the width of it, travel the length of it, soar to its heights and plumb its depths. The love of the Father, which is in Christ Jesus, poured out by His Holy Spirit. This is what we are coming into. When God said to me, "I am laying a new foundation of love in My Church," *this* is what He is talking about. This is what He is doing on the earth today. This is not confined to a group or a movement – it is happening everywhere. There is a tsunami wave of love building out in the ocean, and it is gaining momentum. There is an underground movement that is not immediately obvious to the casual observer. When the wave hits, it will be a mighty wave that breaks upon us all. This wave, this tsunami wave, is the love of the Father. It is inexorable and relentless because it flows from His heart.

The most remarkable thing about my experience of the cloud was this: this was an unprecedented experience full of love and revelation, and there was so much of the miraculous activity of the Spirit happening in the room ... yet ... we were *not* in the cloud.

Let me repeat that. *We were not in the cloud.* I was observing this cloud as it was beginning to move from the back of the room, like a mist seeping from the walls but it hadn't even begun to envelop us.

What struck me forcefully was this. Love was there in the room – but we were still not in it! So many amazing things were going on – yet we were *outside* the cloud. At best, we were on the periphery of the cloud of love but we hadn't even begun to enter it. We had an incredible sense of His presence and His being but we couldn't enter into it because we weren't strong enough. We needed to be strengthened in our inner being so that we could know the love. Our spirits needed to be expanded to even contain a drop of this love.

This is the process that God has us in at this present time. It is a process of being strengthened in our inner being so that we might be able to comprehend *the* love. Some of us are only at the beginning. Like newborn babes we are learning how to drink drop by drop, little by little. Every now and then we get what fills us, according to the heart capacity that we have, but then we get dry and thirsty. But as we stay in that place of hungering, thirsting and desiring Him, we are discovering what it is to live in Him and to feed on His life.

7 | Receiving the Love
A meditation

If there is one reality that I know it is this – Father wants to come in a very tangible way to *all of us*. He wants to come into the deep regions of our hearts. He wants us to be rooted and established in the rich soil of His nurturing love. Rooted and grounded in this real and nurturing love that was His original intent for us to possess and live in. He knows you. He knows more about you that *you* do. Things that you have forgotten, He remembers. He has seen you. He has heard the baby or young child who cries out in the dark when nobody wants to answer and bring reassuring comfort.

He has seen the aloneness. He has seen the times when you came home from school and you needed loving arms to embrace you, drawing you into the haven of home. When you needed to hear words that spoke life into you after you had been teased and tormented, put down or perceived to have failed. He has desired that you would come home to the place where there were arms to receive you, and a smile that says, "You are the best!"

He has seen it all and He knows how much you need Him. He knows how much you need a mother's nurturing love.

Where you are right now you can just relax and become that little child. As much as you can do it, just relax and be a little child. Inside us all is a little boy or a little girl that really needs to be loved. Right now, in the place where you are, you can access and receive this. You can be in that place of peace.

King David said in Psalm 131, "I have weaned and quieted my soul like a well-fed child upon its mother's breast." The weaning that he speaks of here is not the weaning off the breast, but rather it refers to a child who has just finished feeding and who is totally satiated to the point of being 'drunk' with its mother's milk. With all the responsibilities of his kingship, he was able to come to a place of peace in the arms of God.

The apostle Paul had a foundation of comfort within his life. After his conversion on the Damascus road he spent three years in the deserts of Arabia. I believe that he was learning to receive comfort from the Father. There is one thing about a religious fanatic (which Paul undoubtedly had been) and it is that they have never received comfort. In his second letter to the Corinthians, however, Paul begins by praising the "God and Father of the Lord Jesus Christ", who he describes as being, "the God of all comfort." He goes on to talk about how he has been comforted by that love so much that it overflowed to others. This affected his whole life and his ministry, both of which were characterised by gentleness, " ... like a mother caring for her little children." Paul knew experientially the mother heart of God and it was liberally manifested in his own life.

Dear friend, the Holy Spirit can come to your neediness and administer the reality of the Father. We *know* that we are desperately needy. We know deep down on the inside that something is missing. We feel so inadequate. So many of us needed to be held in the night. Our hearts so longed to hear our mother's voice sing a gentle lullaby over us. What a difference it would have made!

If only we had a mother who hadn't been destroyed by the things in her life. A mother that could have sung endearing words to us – that could have wiped our brow. If only we had a mother that could have said, "You are safe. Let me hold you tenderly." If only you could have felt the softness of her body and the warmth of her affectionate love, and breathed the sweet smell of her breath.

CR

Father comes to us, beloved. He comes as a tender mother. There is no condemnation in Him. He has seen the things we have struggled with and the temptations we have faced. He knows the deeply embedded shame in our hearts because of who we are and the things that we just cannot shake off.

He understands and wants to come to us in this very moment to be a mother to us. He is the Breasted One! He looks deep into our eyes – through the window of the soul into the very deepest part of us. He pours His liquid love deep into our souls. He smiles at us and we hear Him say, "You are perfect. Perfect! There is no flaw in you, My darling child." He whispers to us that we are welcome here, that we are so precious to Him.

Dear ones, we are the delight of His heart. There are no limits to His love for you. There are no limits at all. All the limits have completely evaporated because He is intent on loving us into life. Let peace like a river flow – rest where there has been no rest. Break off the fear of love. Many have feared the very idea of being loved because they equate it with being smothered, with being unable to breathe. If that is you, I can reassure you – what you have thought of as being 'love' has not been the pure love of the Father's intention. You were created *to be loved* – not to be smothered. You were made to be *set free* in love. The Father's love sets you free. Jesus has set you free to *be* free without limits in the Father's love.

Some have never been able to open up their hearts and trust but Father is giving us the ability to trust. The black hole of desolation and abandonment now becomes a safety net that you can fall into.

Come to the breast of El Shaddai. If you have never been held to the breast you can be in that place that King David knew so well – the place of vulnerability and the place of strength. That may sound like a paradox but in the Father's love vulnerability and strength can co-exist together without tension. In fact, there is no real strength without vulnerability. Vulnerability is the open point of access to the Father's strengthening nourishment.

The Father can open up a capacity to let us experience the love that surpasses understanding – the love that is greater than all knowledge – the love deeper than the deepest ocean, higher than the highest mountain – reaching up to the clouds and beyond. The Father has given us grace to believe in Him. He has given us grace to come to that place in His heart that is open to us.

As a little baby lies helpless in its mother's arms, He wants us to be before Him – to drink from His milk and to be nourished and given life.

෧෬

Father is here! He says, "I have created you to live, to be, to belong, to be part of My creation. I have created you to be part of My family in order that you may be one with Me. I am calling you to life. I am calling back through your generations. I am calling back through those ones that turned their hearts against Me, who said, "I cannot believe in a God like that!" I am calling back beyond that generation that the life that was in Christ might break through. A different life! A life that has another Source! A life greater than an earthly life. And this Life calls to you, "My daughter, My son!" Greater than any reality that this earth has known, is this life that I call you into. Live! Live!"

There are those that have been rejected and abandoned. There are those – even before their conscious mind had an opportunity to know what it was doing – whose spirit said, "I do not want you!" There is deep abandonment for some. The Father will come and give grace that has never been present before. He will give grace to that person who rejected their mother's incapacity to love and to want them, and who in turn have said, "Neither do I want you!" Father sees us and comes! The prophet Ezekiel says in Chapter 16:4-7:

> *On the day you were born your cord was not cut, nor were you washed with water to make you clean, nor were you rubbed with salt or wrapped in cloths. No one looked on you with pity or had compassion enough to do any of these things for you.*

The Father wants to go deep to that moment of birth. He wants to minister to that very point of your need.

> *Rather, you were thrown out into the open field, for on the day you were born you were despised.*

There has been a lie that has penetrated deep into the heart. Right from the moment of birth – and even conception – there were those who knew instinctively that they were despised and rejected.

> *Then I passed by and saw you kicking about in your blood, and as you lay there in your blood I said to you,*

"Live!" I made you grow like a plant of the field. You grew up and developed and became the most beautiful of jewels. Your breasts were formed and your hair grew, you who were naked and bare.

There has been such a deep shame about your whole existence – even your whole being – but He passes by and says, "Live!" His love calls you into newness of life. The word for you is, "Live!"

So many have been so aware that they are naked and bare, and have sought to hide themselves away. They have tried many things to cover the nakedness and the shame.

He has come to us as a mother, to pick up this "little one" and to look deep into her eyes so that she would know the smile that comes from His heart. He is the Father of Life who causes us to live. All life emanates from Him and He is here to mother us, to nurture us, to bring us into the fullness of the life that He has – the life that He ordained for us before the foundations of the world. He is like a mother who weeps over her children, who weeps because they do not know her love and her care and who weeps because they cannot receive it.

ᘓ

No one has the love of a mother like Father God. He gives us the reality of belonging. He comes with the sword of the Spirit into the deep, dark place of abandonment. The mother rises up with a motherly fierceness and protectiveness. Like a lioness or a she-bear she is outraged against what has come against this one whom she loves so dearly. With that sword the torment is cut off and the lies are severed – to break the power of the falsehood that you are not wanted, that you have no destiny, that you have no right to life.

Jesus came that you might have abundant and over-flowing life. He came that you would know the reality of this comforting heart. This mothering love that sings over Jerusalem, that sings for joy over *you*. No lie is strong enough to overcome this life, or to overcome this love! Neither height nor depth, nor things to come, nor things that are past, no angel or demon can separate you from this love that is in His mother's heart for *you* belong there.

You were conceived and grew in the womb before you were ever born again. You were in the womb of the Spirit, conceived in love, nurtured, then born again into a life that has no darkness. There is no genealogy in this world that is more powerful than the genealogy that you have come into in Christ.

So many people, both men and women, have had their femininity stolen from them. There has been no one to call them into life, no one to look into their eyes and say, "I love you. You are the most important and precious gift. You are the greatest miracle I have ever seen."

☙

God is loving you right now, welcoming you into life. Father God in His mothering love is with you right now. Little eyes that have never seen the light are beginning to blink. When a baby is first born their little eyes open to bright lights. They open for a second then shut and then open again. They become accustomed to the light and look around, then they settle on the mother's breast and from there all that their eyes can see is mother's eyes looking back down at them, seeing their perfection.

Father says, "You are perfect!" There is no limit and no end to His mothering love. It requires nothing of us but 'to be' – just 'to be' because you are perfect as you are. He has come to our lonely nights and to the times when there has been violence within and around us. He is here to mother us, to comfort us. He *is* our comforter. He is not merely *a* comforter, He is *the* comforter, pouring in His love, singing songs over us and bringing us into that new place, that deep place where we have never dared to feel that we belong. He lovingly brings us there!

We can look up at Him as we come into this place of new birth, as it were. We can look up and see that big smile that says, "You are so beautiful. My heart breaks with your beauty and the perfection that I am seeing. You are perfect and without flaw in My sight."

ॐ

Beloved, it is better than we ever dared to believe! He pours liquid love into those places that have been so cold. His mothering love is so deep and goes to the very core of who we are. Deep calling unto deep.

He takes away all fear. The fear of being loved is such a deep fear. But He is the lover of our souls. His love removes all the fear that has made us so vulnerable to pain. His love comes to that very place where we have opened our hearts to love and have been so rejected. To that very place of pain and rejection His love comes. Where our trust has been broken, He restores.

His love is gracious and compassionate. It is like a deep, unfathomable ocean, the mother-love of God! His love is so strong and yet it is so gentle and tender, so exquisite. It has a heart-warming smile that melts away the coldness in your heart.

His comfort-love brings a deep cleansing into the places of defilement where we have looked for love in the wrong places. His love covers all of that. It cleanses and heals and makes new. It makes the desert spring forth and waters the dry places. New life, new growth, new joy! All things have become new! We have a joy that is rooted in the fact that He will never leave us. Never!

We have been born into a love that has no limits and that is infinitely greater than any earthly love. Love without limits and boundaries. God will always love you! Father has always and will always love you. His love and peace will flow like a river – a deep impartation enough for a city, enough for a nation! You can receive that love now!

Bibliography

Bushnell, Katharine C. *God's Word to Women,* Reprint. Ed. Eagle Lake, TX: GWTW Publishers, 2004.

Cantalamessa, Raniero. *Life in Christ: A Spiritual Commentary on the Letter to the Romans*, Collegeville, MN: The Liturgical Press, 1990.

Guyon, Madame Jeanne. *Union with God,* Reprint Ed. Goleta, CA: Christian Books, 1981.

Hyatt, Susan C. *In the Spirit We're Equal: The Spirit, The Bible and Women - A Revival Perspective*, Tulsa OK: Hyatt Press, 1998.

John Paul II, Pope. *The Theology of the Body: Human Love in the Divine Plan,* Boston, Pauline Books and Media, 1997.

Johnson, Darrell W. *Experiencing the Trinity,* Vancouver: Regent College Publishing, 2002.

Kreeft, Peter. *C S Lewis for the Third Millennium*, San Francisco: Ignatius Press, 1994.

Kreeft, Peter. *Heaven: The Heart's Deepest Longing (Expanded Edition)*, San Francisco: Ignatius Press, 1989.

Kristof, Nicholas D. & Wudunn, Sheryl. *Half the Sky: How to Change the World*, London: Virago Press, 2010.

Lake John G. *The Complete Collection of His Life Teachings (complied by Roberts Liardon)*, New Kensington, PN, Whitaker House, 1999.

Lewis, C.S. *A Grief Observed,* London: Faber and Faber, 1961.

Lewis, C.S. *Perelandra*, Reprint Ed. London: HarperCollins Publishers, 2005.

Lewis, C.S. *The Four Loves*, Reprint Ed. London: Fount, 1998.

Lewis, C.S. *The Weight of Glory and Other Addresses,* Reprint Ed. New York: HarperCollins, 2001.

Nee, Watchman. *The Glorious Church: God's View Concerning the Church,* Anaheim, CA: Living Stream Ministry, 1993.

Nouwen, Henri J.M. *The Inner Voice of Love: A Journey Through Anguish to Freedom,* New York: Doubleday, 1996.

Tournier, Paul. *The Gift of Feeling (Translation of: La Mission de la Femme),* Atlanta, GA: John Knox Press, 1979.

Tournier, Paul. *What's in a Name? (Translation of: Quel nom lui donnerez-vous?)*, London: SCM Press Ltd., 1975.

Vanier, Jean. *Becoming Human,* Toronto: House of Anansi Press Ltd., 1998.

Vanier, Jean. *Community and Growth (English Edition),* Sydney: St. Paul Publications, 1979.

Vanier, Jean. *Man and Woman He Made Them (English Edition)*, Sydney: St. Paul Publications, 1985.